SO MANY WAYS TO DIE

SURVIVING AS A SPY IN THE SKY

BY R. SCOTT BEAT, US NAVY, RETIRED

IN COLLABORATION WITH DR. JERRIE NEWMAN

First published by Dog Ear Publishing
4010 W. 86th Street, Ste H
Indianapolis, IN 46268
www.dogearpublishing.net

ISBN: 978-159858-276-5
Library of Congress Control Number: 2006940595

This book is printed on acid-free paper.

Printed in the United States of America

DEDICATION

This book is dedicated to my wife, Jan, whose love, trust and faith have never wavered through the multitude of my scheduled and sometimes unexpected absences of indeterminate durations.

Military wives and families are seldom lauded for their patience and dedication. Only military wives who have lived such lives of uncertainty and self-sacrificing devotion can truly relate to and fully comprehend what is involved.

ACKNOWLEDGMENTS

This book from its inception has been a work in progress for more than six years. Numerous friends and aviation associates proffered technical information, advice and research assistance for which I am grateful.

One friend more than others was especially helpful. Dr. Jerrie Newman, my editor and co-author, of Camarillo, California, gave generously of her time to assist with her computer skills, manuscript work, and literary talent. Her invaluable research, writing, and professional counseling aided the author in adhering to the centerline of his narrative goals. Another friend, Fred Baskin, scanned and modified all of the pictures included with the text. I am eternally grateful to both.

THE OPINIONS OF OTHERS

Major Craig Loe says,

As commander of the US Army Security Agency team involved in the joint project SEABRINE, I had the privilege to work and fly with LCDR Scott Beat as the Squadron Project Officer and primary aircraft commander. During my tour of duty, I had the opportunity to fly in the project aircraft with a number of squadron aviators, all of whom I felt were highly qualified professional US Navy aviators. At no time did I experience a lack of confidence in their abilities to take the aircraft, with my Army crew aboard, to the usually risky operational location, and return us safely to base.

However, when Scott Beat was our aircraft commander on a mission operation, I personally felt an additional measure of personal safety and comfort for myself and my men. Scott seemed to have an extraordinary feel for the aircraft, the machine responding to his commands as if it were a well trained bird. It was as if the aircraft became the duty uniform of the day he was wearing. Thirty years after the experience, I would still be willing to fly with Scott any time any place…*Major Craig Loe*

Jack Poss, Flight Engineer, says,

As Commander Beat's Flight Engineer, I had opportunities to fly with him during many stressful situations. He was a very proficient pilot who always kept his thoughts way out ahead of his aircraft which allowed him to anticipate situations before they became serious problems. He was definitely the pilot to be with if one had an over abundance of adrenalin. :"The Boss" was a MIG and missile magnet. Eighty five percent of the missions I flew with him in the latter part of 1965 attracted missiles and MIG's. Commander Beat's pilot proficiency was consistently excellent—even under combat and airborne emergency situations. Carrier pilots are, in my prejudiced opinion, simply the best the military has and Scott Beat was close to the top of the list. It's easy to prove. He always brought his aircraft and aircrew home safely.

from My Life Around Airplanes by Matthew A. Nelson, (available on-line)

"Within a few days of arriving back at Atsugi, I had the distinct pleasure and memory of going on my first flight of PR-9, the EA-3B, Navy

Bureau number 146449. The Douglas Aircraft Company built this aircraft, and the Air Force equivalent was called the B-66. Normally, the plane was called an A-3, which was initially designed as a bomber, but the bomb bay was modified and an electronics compartment substituted in its place, hence, the first letter, E. PR-9 had a crew of seven, which consisted of the Pilot, Navigator-Bombardier, a Navy enlisted man who was the plane captain, and four army guys who flew in the back manning the electronics equipment.

"Commander Scott Beat piloted the plane on my first flight. Near the end of our four-hour mission, CDR Beat called me to the cockpit and gave me a briefing. Then he performed a barrel roll over Mt. Fuji. He timed it so that I was standing upside down looking directly into the crater of Mt. Fuji. That was one of the best plane rides of my life! Thanks, Commander Beat.

As far as I am concerned, CDR Scott Beat is one of the best aviators that the Navy ever produced.

Once, we had a couple of MIGS' intercept and fly near us. CDR Beat told us not to even look at them and not to wave or anything…since we were unarmed. On a previous mission, before I joined the 1st SAD, there was another intercept, and it was said that the Russian pilots were begging their ground control people for permission to shoot down our plane." (1st SAD was a Special Activities Detachment of the Army.)

Editor's Note: During the writing of this book, Scott Beat often expressed to me the wonder that he was the one of those who survived. Aviation accidents—a tail hook that didn't catch the arresting cables, a catapult launch that malfunctioned, a carrier that pitched at night in bad weather, aircraft equipment that suffered airborne malfunctions, fuel leaks, engine oil leaks, hydraulic leaks, electronic failures, airborne combat damage—so many ways and combinations that could and did confound the finest pilots and render them helpless at the mercy of a cruel fate to remove them from parents, wives, children—and the fascination of flying: many of these he experienced, and yet he was spared.

He attributed his "luck" to a personal propensity—quietly imprinted on his mind by a cautious and caring father—to assess risks and anticipate outcomes. No matter how often he climbed into an aircraft, he was never cavalier about check lists. No matter how often he soared to high altitudes, he was never careless. No matter how often he approached the deck of the speck of an aircraft carrier in the spanning ocean, he never skipped procedures.

He flew because he loved the soaring enchantment of endless space and the blurring speed when his aircraft and he became one indivisible unit and the skin of the bird became an extension of himself; but even when Scott marveled and soared, responding to the ecstasy of private joy, he was always aware that practical protocols, drilled by the Navy flight instructors, were rules of the game to be scrupulously followed.

He seemed to become two beings in one brain—one clicked off the list of potential dangers and practical ways to avoid them; the other circled the blue earth globe from horizon to horizon and sang the glory of flight.

He seemed to be born to fly; he was a "natural." From the moment he flew his first single engine trainer, he simply "knew" how to fly. By the time he was awarded his 20th Air Medal for surveillance over the hostile Pacific arena in unarmed reconnaissance aircraft, he had become one of the best pilots the Navy had.

He is unusually modest about his ability and accomplishments.

He simply says, "If you are truly an excellent aviator, boasting is just hot air. Other pilots know."

The majority of air crewmen who flew with Scott were as relaxed as the situations could permit. They recognized the learned and instinctive talent Scott had. He possessed the ability to coax maximum response and performance from the metal tonnage that ignored the laws of gravity and flew.

One air crewman who had flown with Scott said it most succinctly. "You don't fly that aircraft. You wear it!"—and he did.

Another factor was Scott's faith in his divine creator. He was unashamedly aware of a presence that he could call on when needed. When he had "luck," it was not all chance; he was aware of the comforting, supporting hand beneath him and his aircraft. Though not devout in a church attending sense, he walked through the shadows as if in a circle of light, confident of a higher being to be beseeched in crisis. God was always there for him and responded to his most urgent prayers.

"I never thought I'd make it home alive," he says simply.

So "skill" and "luck" could also be called "talent" and "God."

However it came to pass, it made for an extraordinary life adventure by an American Naval Aviation Warrior. He loyally served his nation with intrepid courage and dedication for more than two decades—through three wars and a half dozen armed international crises.

And he survived!

Dr. Jerrie Newman, co-author and editor

Table of Contents

CHAPTER 1—

SO MANY WAYS TO DIE

Some survived; some died.
Sometimes it was skill; sometimes it was luck.

There were so many ways to die.

Simple accidents: A careening car on a slick highway;…a truck that backed up at the wrong time;…stomach disorders from strange bacteria in foreign lands;…a cold that became pneumonia…an explosion…a sniper's bullet.

Then there were the other ways, those that pilots feared:…Plane engines that malfunctioned;…tail hooks that didn't catch;…birds that fouled the intakes;…empty fuel tanks;…leaking oil;…fighter planes screeching out of the sky;…uncontrollable, changeable weather that tossed a plane like a toy.

Any pilot who boasted that he was not afraid was simply a liar. We all took all the precautions we could and trusted to our training, our reaction time, and sheer dumb luck.

Some were luckier than others.

Even the wives of Navy pilots had to endure the specter of death.

In an early deployment in Florida, my wife Jan had to learn what it meant to be a Navy wife. She was no longer simply Jan Paulson Beat, a sensitive, accomplished, college graduate, kindergarten teacher from a good family. Now she had to become part of the "Yes, Sir!" culture that I had learned years before.

It was demanding, often demeaning. Happy Hour at five each Friday was obligatory. White gloves, hats, and calling cards *de rigueur*. At wives' teas, the commanding officer's wife snapped orders: "My girls will spend three hours a week at Navy Relief." And they did!

Jan had signed no contract, but she, too, was in the Navy!

One consolation was good friends from the Annapolis years. Sara and

Buck Sheeley, Bernie and Diane Joyce, and Milton and Marge Lucas lived nearby and were part of the tight social circle that developed there.

Diane and Jan were at an officers' wives' coffee one fateful day, when Diane was called out and gently informed by the Skipper's wife that Bernie had died practicing mirror landings—landings that simulated the tight boundaries of a carrier landing. Jan had to drive Diane home, numbing sorrow a palpable silent presence in the car.

Just as I had been thrust into maturity when I early on witnessed an accidental death, now Jan had to face the reality that a Skipper or his wife might some day call her out with dreadful news, and that she would be expected to accept that I was gone and she was a widow. Sudden death was a part of any Navy flying career.

Our friend Milton Lucas was also later to tragically die when the cold catapult that all carrier pilots feared, the catapult which should have lofted his aircraft into the air, failed, and his aircraft dribbled off the end of the carrier which unstoppably rode over him and his aircraft.

Another friend, Carl Austin, was lost when his terrain avoidance radar didn't work near Hanoi, and he plowed into a mountain.

Dan Beard, a classmate at Annapolis and a neighbor when we lived in Sanford, Florida, flew into a mountain in Vietnam. His aircraft had so much secret equipment aboard that a special armed search party was sent in, not to bring out the bodies, but to bring out or destroy the equipment. I had to help his wife with routine problems after his death. It was a constant reminder that I could be next.

The Navy lost a total of 67 air wing commanders, squadron commanders, and squadron executive officers in combat during the air operations in the Vietnam War. More than half of all the combat sorties flown into North Vietnam were by Naval aircraft.

I came close to death so often, and yet it passed me by and allowed me a gracefully long life span. I was daring, but careful, and my caution often brought me and my crew safely out of the sky. However, there was one occasion when I came so close—when no skill was involved. Simply luck.

I had been flying with VQ-1 out of Atsugi, Japan to detachments in DaNang for about five years. My assigned task was to pilot one of the eleven EA3B Skywarriors, (affectionately known as "The Whale") on reconnaissance flights to support the war fighters. This was a carrier based jet with a crew of electronic experts: a navigator, cryptology technicians

(CTs) who handled classified, time-sensitive mission communications, and a team of enlisted operators who sat at a bank of monitors and electronic equipment on the starboard side of the plane. This included avionics technicians or aviation electricians called electronic warfare operators whose function it was to detect and locate electronic emissions by a target nation, aircraft or ship.

These planes were in the air 24-7, and I, or other pilots like me, could be sent out on as many as four flights in a 24 hour period. Three flights were common.

The information we collected went into a central database and to fleet commanders to inform them of enemy activity. It also went to strike pilots to alert them to any enemy that possibly targeted them.

Ours was a relatively small operation compared to the much larger land-based EC-121, which had been introduced in 1966 as state-of-the-art aircraft that could transmit results directly to the main control center at DaNang. The EC-121 was an unarmed propeller-driven aircraft that carried six tons of electronics equipment. The aircraft was able to direct fighter escort operations that had been tasked with intercepting any enemy aircraft that threatened the strike packages. It could also provide rescue and navigation assistance to searches for downed aircrews and helped fighters who were low on fuel to locate tankers. They flew even longer than we, up to 12 hours.

Being insatiably curious, I'd always wanted to fly in the EC-121, so in March, 1969, when a good friend of mine, LCDR James Overstreet, who was the aircraft commander on PR-21, caught up with me in Atsugi and told me he'd be going out the next day, it didn't take a second invitation.

The next morning, I suited up and was ready to go out on the flight. I climbed aboard and looked for an unassigned seat. However, Jim, at the last minute, called me to the cockpit and apologized

"We just recomputed our weight and balance sheet." He said reluctantly. "We're overloaded with a crew of 31 and I just can't take you on this flight. I promise I'll get in touch you later!"

I was, of course, disappointed but fully expected to go out on another run.

Luck was with me that day—supreme good fortune.

I heard about the course of Jim's flight later.

For the first routine seven hours of the flight, Overstreet followed an elliptical, clockwise course around the Sea of Japan. Then, a ground station in South Korea radioed a warning that two North Korean MIG jet fighters had taken off from a base normally used only for training and were headed toward the EC-121. Overstreet acknowledged the message and turned the aircraft seaward from a position well outside the 12 mile limit claimed by North Korea, planning to end the mission and return to Atsugi.

On the monitoring radars in Japan and South Korea, the blips of the North Korean jets and the EC-121 met and passed. The American plane disappeared from the screen and was not heard from again.

It had been only 15 months since the USS Pueblo was captured by the North Koreans, so the Navy dispatched carriers Enterprise, Ticonderoga, Ranger, and Hornet in the task force TF-71. There were a total of 40 ships: four carriers, three cruisers, 22 destroyers, five submarines, 6 supply ships, and for a time the battleship New Jersey.

It was an international crisis!

The National Security Agency (NSA) later determined that the cause of the shoot down was a command and control error between the North Korean ground controller and the MIG fighter pilot. It was an accident. Even Russian warships were sent to help search for survivors. An extensive search found only wreckage and the bodies of two men, 90 miles off the coast of Korea.

All 31 men were lost.

I would have been one of them, had I been on the aircraft. I knew Jim Overstreet, Lt. Dennis B. Gleason, Lt. John H. Singer, and CT3 Philip D. Sundby. All good men. All abruptly gone.

Why I lived, in this case, when so many others died had nothing to do with skill.

It was pure luck, and part of the reason I am here today and able to write of my close encounters with death.

The pilot in this AD6 was one of the lucky ones. Lt. jg Bob Brace flew off the deck of the USS Yorktown (CVA-10). He added full power and engine torque twisted the plane so he went off the side and curled into the ocean. A plane guard helicopter rescued him.

CHAPTER 2—

THE RISK TAKER

My father held out his hand to my mother.
"He can't help himself," he said. He's a born risk taker."

My parents, Manda and John Beat, lived in a three story brick house near the edge of town, where Mt. Horeb, with its squared Midwestern streets, gave way to the rolling hills and emerald meadows of Wisconsin dairy land. In winter, these same Dane County hills became white crested ridges of icy drifts. Summer brought black clouds of pesky mosquitoes and heat and humidity in the 90's, but, as if in recompense, chartreuse spring waved its wild flowers of rebirth and crisp fall flashed overnight to a glorious red and gold extravagance and the pungent smoke of burning leaves.

It was a safe town, where children could run free and people did not lock their doors.

My father had built the house on land given him by his father—part of a parental invitation to forsake a career as an electrical engineer in favor of co-ownership of the hardware store along with brother Roy. My father had graduated from the University of Wisconsin, made his quiet decision, and never played the game of "might-have-been." Life with my mother, my two brothers and I, was good. He was content.

I heard the story often, a part of the oral history of our family, laughed about at Thanksgiving dinners, retold when the cousins gathered, repeated, often to my embarrassment, before the parents of my adolescent girl friends.

My mother stood at the frosted window of their bedroom, the curtain pushed aside, unseeing, gazing over the front porch roof toward the three smaller wooden houses on the other side of Wilson Street and the ice slicked Washington Street hill blocked off for sledding. She was pretty—small and neat, with almost black hair, but with the blue eyes of her Norwegian heritage.

"I so worry about him," she said. Her brow furrowed. "He's so daring."

My dad, on their bed, nodded. He worried too, but without words, as was his wont.

I was their youngest son, Bobby, their treasured towheaded blue-eyed "surprise" who had arrived eight years after Jay and nine years after Lowell, and I was always the subject of their loving concern.

"He jumped off the sleeping porch today, into a snow bank," she sighed. "There's a cement sidewalk under it. It's 30 feet down. He could have died."

I can imagine his calm response, unperturbed as was his wont.

"I know. I talked to him about it. He said the snow was deep enough. He'd looked first." He paused. "He said he wanted to know how it felt to fly."

"He's only six…just a baby."

John held out his hand, inviting her to join him under the quilts. "He can't help himself. He's a born risk taker."

"He almost drowned on the lake spillway last summer."

"He thinks well," John said quietly, snapping off the light by the bed. "We'll have to guide him…teach him to be careful."

Manda sighed. She trusted my father's judgment, just as I learned later to do. "He's so adorable. My little Bobby—my bad Bobby Beat."

I was to become what she predicted and what my father modified: a risk taker, venturesome and sometimes reckless—pulling stunts that gave me a reputation in Mt. Horeb for crazy mischief—but always with a sense of caution prompted by the internalized sound of my father's voice….

Daring…but careful. And alive.

CHAPTER 3—

HERE COMES THE NAVY

Early in 1945 my parents drove me to Milwaukee,
where I signed up for a minority cruise,
the tour of service to begin before I became 18—on April 15—and to
end on my 21st birthday.

When I was ten, after my grandfather had come to spend his final, shuffling years with us, two Robert Beats in one household became confusing. As the one with lesser seniority, I was driven to the Dane County Court House and, with the snapping shut of a ledger book, became a young and yearning Scott Beat, putting in my time and wondering, as all young men do, what to do with my life. I had about decided to plan a career in criminology, in the glamour of F.B.I. labs where I would become famous solving complicated cases with my science and math skills.

Then the Navy called instead!

Mt. Horeb High School had often bored me. The best part about school was the camaraderie of my gang: Billy Johnson, Buster Finke, Vernon Anderson, Wesley Sale, and Burl Eveland. There was a corresponding gaggle of girls: Jane Nelson, Mary Jane Hoff, Joyce and Lucille Thompson, Janet Paulson and Corrine "Corky" Kittleson.

The worst part was the lack of challenge. I studied, but not too hard, since it wasn't necessary. I breezed through the first three years of classes with good grades, and to ward off the boredom, took extra classes, beyond the requirements. By the end of my junior year, I had enough credits to graduate, but the principal told me I would need to put in the time and not be allowed to graduate until the end of the next year. I was too young to join the armed services.

I discovered—from Miss Scaife's classes—English literature and public speaking and poetry—and I memorized long passages that seemed meaningful, passages I can quote to this day.

At Bergh's Bakery or Olson's Restaurant, the girls would giggle in the next booth over, and at night after the boys discovered beer, I would opt out and go home when the others binged, choosing to follow my parents' restraint. My father had made wine but locked it in the basement and brought it out only for special occasions.

I didn't dance and shrugged off my senior prom. I was a young, non-smoking straight arrow, honest to a fault and innocent as only a decent, small town boy can be. You might consider me a slow learner, but I lived by a moral code that is with me yet.

In the sixth grade I had been such a terror that I drove the teacher to leave the Mt. Horeb system. I had led my gang in pranks that kept the town buzzing.

The one time Wesley Sale and I tried cigarettes of corn silk, in seventh grade, I got so dizzy I fell out of a tree and ever after wondered how any-one could "enjoy" puffing away. That was the year that my teacher, Lewis Wainwright made me a monitor in the library, to give me my first taste of leadership. It was intoxicating power that infected me with the need to help guide others.

I was still known to town elders as "Bad Bobby." Women clucked and men chuckled over the bag of wet manure that had somehow dropped—years before—from the highway overpass on the car of Oliver Lee, the town's cop.

My relatively innocent escapades hadn't stopped. With high school, they simply changed character: teaching less inventive friends how to slide down an outside drain to cut classes, speeding across the rolling ribbons of undulating roads in my father's car; pushing over isolated outhouses; caus-ing confusion in the high school study hall; discovering the joy that a woman could bring.

I had a girl friend, Carol Rue, a cute blonde, but we argued inces-santly. We would hang out with friends at Haig's soda shop or go to Olson's Restaurant with its 15 foot tall tin ceilings.

World War II was winding down, but my older brother Lowell had been battling through the Pacific with Macarthur's 32nd Army Division in the Philippines and New Guinea, and my other brother Jay was fighting with Patton through Europe, so the pull of the services was strong. Other boys, only slightly older than I, had gone to the war and returned as men with tales of travel and adventure before again disappearing from tranquil Mt. Horeb.

I felt restless, as if life was sliding by.

Since most able bodied males were away at war, my father put me to work in the family hardware store and quietly suggested that I get training as a plumber, so I studied, passed the tests, and was then a licensed Assistant Plumber who went out on jobs with a colorful master plumber, Frank Sabanski, who swore a profane blue streak—more descriptive than anything I was to hear in 27 years in the Navy—and often chewed on a stinking cigar that dangled from the corner of his mouth. Or we would be out in subzero weather replacing the frozen pipe from the earth below a farmer's windmill.

My father kept me busy, but nothing was enough.

I began a polite campaign to convince my parents that it was time to go to the Navy. I took long, thoughtful, learning walks with my father in the woods around the town, and eventually, when my father had imbued a cautionary message in my immaturely daring mind, Dad and Mom reluctantly agreed that I could join the Navy.

Early in 1945 they drove me to Milwaukee, where I signed up for a minority cruise, the tour of service to begin before I became 18—on April 15—and to end on my 21st birthday. I was excited. A physical. A uniform that I couldn't wait to wear!

The uniform didn't fit, and they sent me home without it to wait out my time. I was let down. It was my first encounter with the impersonal Navy.

Mt. Horeb's seniors graduated on May 24, but in the light of hometown patriotism that waved the flag while it followed the rules, the school administrators granted me the right to a diploma and the right to fight the war.

Before graduation date, I was inducted at Camp Dewey at the Great Lakes Boot Camp where they shaved my butch cut, assigned me a bunk, gave me an ill-fitting uniform, and assigned me to a Chief Petty Officer who became God and the Devil for eight weeks. It was up at dawn, shave, dress, inspection, march to mess hall, look at the bulletin board for the day's schedule.

I saw what happened to those who disobeyed and since I didn't really want to clean latrines, I suppressed my alter-ego, Bad Bobby Beat, and fell in line to become anonymous, obedient Scott Beat who dutifully did his KP rotation.

Before, there had been no real consequences for bad behavior—only tolerant amusement. Now I was in an adult, structured world.

I learned how to fight simulated shipboard oil fires and electrical and chemical fires. I was taught, along with other boot sailors in my company, how to fire 50 caliber machine guns and 40 mm. antiaircraft guns on the restricted Great Lakes Gunnery Range of Lake Michigan, using live ammunition.

We learned to march to cadence barked out by drill instructors on the sun scorched asphalt grinders, or drill fields, and to perform all facets of the military manual of arms with a rifle. In class we learned seamanship, ship identification, military courtesy, military discipline, and a basic understanding of the code of military justice.

I didn't know it then, but the inculcation delved into my very soul and I became Navy for life, from the way I strutted and saluted to the very secret crevices of my brain.

President Franklin D. Roosevelt died. The atomic bomb was dropped on Japan.

The war ended on August 14, 1945.

Here I was, in the Navy with no war to fight.

Upon completion of boot camp, I received orders to report for duty aboard a patrol craft of antisubmarine operations operating under control of the U. S. Navy Panama Canal Authority. Only I was sent—a game piece on a giant board.

It was exciting. Everyone was young. Our commanding officer was a fun-loving Lt. jg; most of my fellow sailors were in their late teens.

The patrol craft was underpowered with only a deck gun and depth charges, but those PC's were designed as an early warning, expendable system, many without radar, whose main task would be a delaying tactic, once the crew visually sighted a sub, sounded an alarm, and then waited for aircraft and/or destroyers to take on the enemy.

The Navy ordered patrol craft to carry out patrols in the Caribbean Sea in close vicinity of Colon, Panama, where sea going vessels entered and exited a waterway to and from the Gatun Locks and the Panama Canal. It was vital that ships not be sunk in the approaches to and from the northeast end of the Canal, sinkings that might inhibit or block the use of this passageway between oceans. The Government had been understandingly concerned that Axis submarines might attempt to torpedo and sink shipping; hence the antisubmarine patrols.

I was one of three sailors assigned to drop the depth charges should the craft encounter a U-boat. The night patrols surged through spooky and scary blind black waters without radar.

But the war was over. So what were we doing there!

The crew wanted to name the patrol craft and requested approval from the Commanding Officer, Lt. (jg.) Black. He thought a moment and then responded, "Absolutely not. But if I don't know about it…and only one small name on the stern!"

After a week of bickering and arguments, the crew unanimously christened the patrol boat as the "USS Chagres Charger" which seemed appropriate since the Chagres River flowed through Gatun Lake and kept it replenished with fresh water, with the river's excess water discharging into the Caribbean Sea.

Our lieutenant used every excuse possible to get us into port to buy fresh fruit to relieve the tedium of c-rations, to walk the streets and ogle the women.

Then out we would go—to fish! We hooked a half inch, 100 ft. manila rope to a cleat on the deck; the Coxswain spliced a clevis with an eight foot braided cable ending with a huge hook baited with salt pork. When a shark struck, we would all grab the line and haul in unison, shouting encouragement, battling a denizen of the deep. With luck we'd get the monster within rifle distance and leave the splattered carcass for waylaying other sharks. Smaller fish would be hauled aboard, but with no cooking facilities, it was catch and release—a months' long fishing cruise. It was war at its finest!

As abruptly as it began, it ended. Orders came through in September of '45. A ship took me to Florida. A train made a multi-change trip to Nebraska and the U. S. Naval Ammunition Depot at Hastings.

Though I didn't know it, Luck had smiled upon me.

Ninety percent of the workers were civilians and the hundreds of Navy personnel were almost a skeleton crew at the 78 square miles of the second largest Naval ammunition depot in the world. With the War now history, the task there was to load and unload outdated ammunition, sort through it, reprocess the usable and demolish the unusable.

The flat, monotonous, wind-swept prairie extended endlessly, interrupted only by lumps of widely-spaced green alien tumors—concrete bunkers covered with eight or more feet of sod. The base was well-established with lawns, plants, and sidewalks. Rail spurs led everywhere to the brick depots and the camouflaged bunkers. Summers were silently hot and winters were grimly cold with fierce, biting winds.

At dawn six days of the week, we young Navy men-of-strong backs

I inherited Chico, the spider monkey, from another sailor at the Navy Ammunition Depot in Hastings, Nebraska. When, in turn, I was transferred out, I passed Chico on.

In less than a year at Hastings, I was promoted from Seaman First Class to Third Class Petty Officer.

would file onto a flat, open-sided trailer behind a semi-tractor and head out in these unheated cattle cars to move pallets of ammunition around as ordered, to store or unstore from the revetments.

I had matured somewhat, but the first sight of sudden, unexpected death appalled me.

I think I grew up that day.

Each concrete revetment had in front of it a lockable, fireproof door. Across the front of this was a concrete platform, the height of a flatbed truck. Our work party was unloading pallets of ammunition from a Navy stake truck, a flat bed with stakes around it.

Something fell off the concrete pad. A sailor shouted, "I'll get it!" and jumped down.

The truck backed up and as the man straightened up, crushed his chest. His ribs cracked like knuckles. Blood spurted from his mouth, ears, and nose. In that moment, he was dead. The warning shouts stopped.

Only the wind and the rumble of distant trucks broke the silence. I was stunned. How could life leave so suddenly, almost without warning!

There was more death to come, but hearing about it and seeing it are different experiences.

Months later, at midnight, in a barrack-rattling explosion, an ammunition depot blew up and every person at work simply disappeared. The only body part found was a part of a hand in a glove. A crater in the ground where a brick building had been was 50 feet deep and 100 feet long.

As nearly as could be reconstructed, a forklift operator had dropped a wheel off of a loading ramp while moving a torpedo warhead. The ensuing fire and explosion set off many tons of torpedo warheads and eight inch naval gun projectiles. It was an instant holocaust!

In spite of this, I volunteered to help destroy obsolete ammunition and underwent a near-deadly initiation. The work crew was at the "Snake Pit" where old, useless ammunition was ignited and destroyed.

"Walk to the edge of the pit," I was told. "Pull the pin on the grenade. Toss it in the pit. And run like Hell!"

The blast threw me 30 feet, while the others roared with laughter. I then learned that the safe, usual method was to run a wire to a considerable distance and detonate a blast with a plunger generator.

I was ambitious. I analyzed the limited potential for advancement in the black shoe Navy and decided that testing was the way up, something I did very well. Now a Seaman First Class, since I could type, I decided to try for Store Keeper as the next step since it was obvious that someone had to keep track of the rail carloads of ammunition that arrived day and night.

The gods now touched me on the shoulder.

I had been assigned to a full lieutenant, one Lt. Cummings, a reservist who had been in the Navy for about six years and was in his late 20's. I never really knew his first name. It was only, "Sir! Yes, Sir, Lieutenant Cummings!"

Cummings had apparently been watching me. I was an "eager beaver" who volunteered for everything, asked questions, and looked alive.

Cummings assigned me as a typist in his office, but the event that triggered my superior's interest came when a cook decided to "borrow" a Navy truck and lead the Shore Patrol on an hours-long chase through the expanses of the ammunition area. The joy-rider avoided capture and returned the Navy gray truck to the dozens of others like it, then vanished. O.K. Where was the truck? Who had taken it on the wild ride? Cummings selected a patrol to check it out and I was among them.

"Sir," I said, suggesting the obvious. "Let's find the one with the hot hood."

Cummings laughed. Within minutes we found the truck. The cook was identified and shipped out.

Cummings called me aside later. "Too many Store Keepers in the Navy already," he advised. "Promotions are frozen. If you're willing to settle for Yeoman, I can use your services."

I studied for the test and earned a Petty Officer's rank and became Yeoman 3rd Class Beat. Cummings apparently continued to watch me and must have been impressed by my gung-ho attitude.

"Would you be interested in trying for Annapolis?"

I didn't even know where Annapolis was.

But a door had been opened to a different world. To become an officer…

All I had ever wanted was to get out of the Navy at 21, go back to school, and become an FBI man.

Cummings formed a three man board of commissioned officers, recusing himself, and the three agreed. "Good officer material here!"

I passed the pass/fail Fleet Screening Exam to qualify for the further Naval Academy screening, was accepted, and in the early summer of '47 was sent back to Great Lakes, since it was the wrong time of the year to begin prepping for the Academy.

My typing skills saved me again, and I was assigned as a typing yeoman for two months to the staff of the Commandant of the 9th Naval District. I passed the Third Class Petty Officer's Exam and got my "crow," and later passed the exam for the Yeoman Second Class, second chevron, but didn't get it because I was slated for Annapolis.

The gods now decided to toy with their freshly minted plaything.

It was too late for entry into the next Annapolis Academy class, so in late summer I, along with 785 other potential material for officers' training, was sent to Bainbridge, Maryland U. S. Training Center to Tome Institute for intensive review in mathematics. School began in earnest: algebra, analytical, and spherical geometry, trigonometry, calculus.

Up at dawn again. Bus to classes. Study. Sleep. Next day the same routine. Only 210 would make it to the Academy.

I was determined I would be one of those chosen ones.

Near the end of the course work, in the winter of '47, I had a flu shot (my last for my lifetime) and immediately came down with a severe case of influenza and was sent to the base hospital with an extremely high fever where a Chief Petty Officer with more gall than brains decided he needed a work detail for a garbage cleanup. I was summoned, along with others in the hospital, from sick bed, and put to work in zero weather stomping around in an inch of evil-smelling, half-frozen swill without proper boots or clothing.

Result: pneumonia that put me in a coma for four days.

Further complication. A medical discharge.

I would not be one of the survivors going for Plebe Summer that year.

All joy vanished in the delivery of that document.

There is a time in the life of many a young man when the path before him drops away, and through a mist of misery, an uncrossable crevasse yawns. On the other side is hope and the future. Here lies despair. I was utterly devastated. I'd done everything right. I'd contained the rebel within me, had conformed, had grown to love the Navy!

How could they do that to me? Just like that! Offer the future and whisk it away. I felt so defeated and rejected, completely helpless for the first time in my life.

An older man, one who had felt the depletion of hope, lived through it, and found another, lesser path to follow, would have trudged stubbornly along, numbed and in pain, but gamely placing one foot before another, with the realization that all things must pass, but a 21 year old must creep silently toward the comforting cave of familiarity and mourn the loss of a bright future and crave for invisibility and privacy.

Everyone at home knew I was headed for Annapolis. Would they understand how I had been slighted? Would they care? All young humans believe that the rest of the world cares enough to observe and question, and only with time do they learn that we are all anonymous, that no one except close family cares, even when we might wish it otherwise.

Back in Mt. Horeb, Mom and Dad were delighted to have me back home again. They understood the depth of my pain. Their tender, loving care and the total acceptance of the townspeople eased my transition back to civilian life. Unbeknownst to me, my dad took quiet control and contacted his Wisconsin area Congressman, Glen Davis.

In these accepting surroundings, I healed quickly in body and mind, began dating a local girl, hung out with my old friends, and searched for another path to follow.

The University of Wisconsin was not far away. My war was over. The Navy was past history, no matter how it hurt to think about it. I would revert to my goal of becoming an FBI man. I enrolled in the Chemical Engineering school the fall of 1948 and took the toughest course they offered. In two winter semesters and the following summer term I took 28 credits to chalk up a 2.85 average and was elected to Phi Eta Sigma. an honorary scholastic fraternity.

Then the gods smiled again, or maybe they smirked.

At any rate, Congressman Davis recommended me for an opportunity to take a Naval Academy entrance exam. I passed easily, and in April, 1949 became a member of the Class of 1953, one year and 2,000 seniority spots later than scheduled. I was to report to Annapolis in June to participate in Plebe Summer along with more than 1300 classmates.

When my appointment came through, pride surged. The deep imprinting came to the fore. I knew then that all I wanted in life was to be a Navy officer.

I was sent to Tome Institute, a school that was like a private college with transient barracks and lots of liberty. By walking a mile or two to a super highway, I could hitchhike into Baltimore. The study—mainly intensive math classes—was challenging but achievable.

The neck of the bottle had narrowed. Of the thousands of candidates who had applied, 1300 would actually attend. Of the 210 from my class from the ill-fated class at Tome Institute, only 100 would make it. Of the 1300 total that entered Plebe Summer, only about 1100 would graduate.

I. Robert Scott Beat, Yeoman 3rd Class, was not only in the Navy. I was a Navy man for life!

CHAPTER 4—

THE MAKING OF A NAVAL OFFICER

That Plebe Year there was never enough time to sleep!
The Navy was parent, director, and controller.
I came to conclude that the system
was brutally and realistically effective.

Plebe year at the Naval Academy at Annapolis was pure Hell.

Every graduate knows it, and not one of them regrets having been through it, but not one of them would live through it twice.

Before my arrival at the Naval Academy in 1949, I felt a little smug. I had come alone by train so that Mom and Dad were not among the clustered parents fluttering away from their nest-grown babies. I had been through boot camp; knew close order drill, handling of arms, and the physical routines. I had regained my confidence as one of the top of my class at the University. I was 22, an experienced Navy man, and many of the Plebes were 18 year old boys straight out of high school.

So that first sweltering, sultry late-June Induction Day as I went through the routines of physical exams, hair cuts, and uniform fitting came as a numbing shock.

"Hup! Two! Don't walk! Run!"

By 1800 hours, when the newly formed companies marched to Tecumseh Court in their new white works and Dixie cups (the white hats of midshipmen) to take the Oath of Office, I was feeling the rigors of the day. Triumph had vanished in a confused jumble of shouted signals and brusque handling.

When morning reveille sounded at 6:15, I woke to realize that this was beyond boot camp, beyond regular Navy, beyond my most radical imaginings.

Wake to a raucous bell—a clanging call that I would come to hate; shave and dress; march to Mess Hall; return to room; march to class; accept that there would be hours of homework every free period and every night; march back to Bancroft Hall; march to Mess Hall; march back to classes; march back to Mother B (as I immediately learned to call Bancroft Hall); study for an hour; march to Mess Hall; march back; study until Tattoo— five minutes before Taps—and lights out at 2155. Twenty-five hours a day studying and doing close order drills with rifles.

Memorize the 3X5 inch, 224 page dark blue Reef Book handed out the first day. Learn how, whom, and when to salute. Commit to memory all the branches of service and their symbols and stripes. Know the history of the Navy, year by year; decorations and honors rankings. Absorb size dimensions and usage of all types of ships and aircraft, their profiles, their symbols, and the line of command aboard. Even the buildings and the monuments! Learn Naval Academy songs and slang. Memorize formulas. Understand concepts. Salute. Compete. Study and regurgitate.

On report with demerits if you didn't conform exactly. (The justification for all this was that the plebes functioned best when obedience was ingrained.)

There was never enough time to sleep. I got an accidental double dose of tetanus and collapsed in front of Bancroft Hall marching to lunch. I welcomed the chance to sleep in sick bay.

I was proud to be a plebe at Annapolis. My roomie and now long time friend Joe Mucka took this shot of me before a Bancroft Hall column

Classes were small—12 to 14 students at wooden chairs with arms for writing—in austere rooms adorned by a blackboard and a desk, designed for up to 30 students for the occasional lecture. Usually a civilian professor.

The section, led by that week's section leader, marched into the classroom single file, stood at attention until the professor entered, then sat in the assigned seats

The Midshipman Brigade had been organized the first day into two regiments, three battalions in each regiment, four companies in each battalion. By chance, I was in the 1st Company of the 1st Battalion of the 1st Regiment. I would know only those in my Company, all housed in the same wing of Bancroft Hall. I lived with them, ate with them, went to class with them, and studied with them.

Plebes in other regiments might well have been on the moon. Acquaintance and close quarters did not often mesh into long-term friendships. Though we shared the same experiences, there wasn't much time for the drawling banter of extended general discussions about life and women, politics and philosophy that is a part of university, college, or fraternity life. When men roomed together for any length of time, they might form close bonds, but, since roommates were assigned, not chosen, compatibility was chancy.

The Navy was parent, director, and controller. When a plebe needed academic help, the small classes made the professor accessible.

A few exceptional young men, who were so sure of their superiority that they needed no apologies, helped other students who were bright—as all plebes were—but who needed help.

Carlyle Trost, who could scan a book and know its smallest secrets, and who later became chief of naval operations, a member of the joint chiefs of staff, and chief of the joint chiefs, was particularly helpful to anyone who asked.

Another helpful plebe, and one of my Plebe Summer roommates, was H. Ross Perot, later to make billions in electronics and run for the Presidency. Though I was near the top of the class in chemical engineering, after two years at the University of Wisconsin, I turned to Perot for help in electronics classes, as did many others.

Perot, a brilliant, personable student, was helpful, asking nothing in return.

During football season, each evening, Perot would wander from room to room during study time, making odds on football pools—and stashing money for himself.

I was fairly good at predicting winners and often came away with ten dollars, an immense sum during those years when a plebe's stipend was $3 a month and uniforms, tailored from Jacob Reed in Philadelphia cost $100 each.

The Academy plan left graduates in debt, unless they were subsidized from home. Firsties—fourth year men—, who by this time had been allowed cars, could not consider such extravagances without family money. Some of the financially privileged plebes, I soon discovered, had been sent to Virginia Military Institute and aimed like missiles for Annapolis. Some had cars, spending money, and no worries. I had chosen the proud Midwestern way and had determined to be fully independent.

After four years, I graduated $200 in debt (the equivalent today of about $4000), but in spite of offers from my parents, I took no money from them.

They later told me the anguish they had felt, along with the pride, knowing the pressures I had endured. Youngsters—second year midshipmen—received $5 a month; Third Year, $9 a month, and Firsties, $13 a month. Without outside help, it was never enough.

George Bancroft, the Secretary of the Navy, whose clever maneuvering had sidestepped Congress to found the Naval Academy in 1845, had set in motion an unstoppable juggernaut that swept up young minds and flattened them into virtual duplicates of each other. In his opening address to the first midshipman class on Oct. 18, 1845, he had emphasized "…a strict compliance with all laws, orders, and regulations." The first superintendent, Commander Franklin Buchanan, a strict disciplinarian, firmly set the pace that was rarely to falter.

Over my four years at the Academy, I came to conclude that the system was brutally and realistically effective. Fear, cloaked in the velvet of pride, kept us midshipmen ever in a state of avoidance. A demerit system, monitored for plebes by the watchful, haughty upper classmen, and administered by unforgiving company officers, punished for the slightest infraction.

A plebe was allowed 300 demerits during the first year.

I received my first five demerits early on, when in a morning rush to meet a time deadline, I left the center desk drawer in my room open one inch.

The next three mornings, at dawn, before the 6:15 reveille, I, along with other wrongdoers, endured three hours of close order drill in full, overheating woolen uniform and white leggings, carrying M-1 rifles at port arms around the 200 yard oval of Warden Field. On the long side of the oval cinder track, the condemned double-timed; on the short section, we walked. By reveille, with a full day ahead, I was fatigued.

There was no forgiveness for any mistake, and I, like all plebes, made many. My room was always immaculate: socks rolled exactly with "smiling faces" exposed; books on the shelf in descending order by height; bed made until a coin bounced.

That summer, I learned that in class, whispering could bring demerits—as could talking in ranks, marching out of step, chewing gum in class or in ranks, not looking straight ahead when marching. Any midshipman whose room was not ready for inspection, who was tardy when falling in for any muster, or whose uniform was not always immaculate in appearance was promptly and effectively punished through the demerit system.

The best of the small pleasures of life that summer were the seamanship classes in the Severn River and Chesapeake Bay. I learned yawls and yachts and scooted around on small motorized boats. I was good at it—a natural sailor.

All this and more became ingrained during that first summer, and my mates and I gained confidence and thought we had it made. Then summer ended and the upper classmen returned.

And the fires of Hell were stoked to livid flame.

Our company commander for the four years at Annapolis was a man named Grkovic who later ran a destroyer aground in the Philippines, and surprised none of us who had suffered under his less than enlightened treatment.

When the men fell in, it was by height, so I,—along with Ross Perot—was at the shorter end of the line. Even when we were marched to the football games, it was by height, which bothered neither me nor the super-confident Perot.

Perot became an Ensign and served for three or four years, then wrote letters of complaint to his Congressman without going through channels and was dismissed from the Navy. However, he was still unfazed and donated millions to build a reception center to name it for a friend who had lost his life in the nation's service.

He and I were friendly acquaintances, nothing more.

The system seemed to discourage the formation of close ties, and of the roommates I had, only one, Joe Muka—who shared the secret embarrassment of grounding a sail boat on Chesapeake Bay—stayed in touch with me over the years.

That first year as a Plebe was survival time.

CHAPTER 5—

ANNAPOLIS: YOUNGSTERS AND BEYOND

I walked Jan back to her sorority dorm and was hit hard:
I was in love…deeply and forever.

Hell was behind us. We were second year men: "Youngsters," in Annapolis parlance.

Eating at mess no longer meant sitting erect exactly two feet back from the table, eating a "square" meal with the fork perpendicular to a 90 degree angle and then horizontally into the mouth all the while perched on the front two inches of the chair. No more subservience to upper classmen. No more squatting on an imaginary "little green stool" until sweat ran down my forehead and my legs trembled. No more confinement to the Yard (the campus) on Saturday and Sundays. No more prohibition of driving in a car with civilians so you ran along side. No more walking the absurd 90 degree turns on an angled path. No more "keeping your eyes in the boat" (straight ahead) and not being allowed to look at, let alone speak to, the beautiful young women who frequented the Yard.

Many of the Youngsters loosed their own sadism on the hapless new Plebes, but I remembered the pain and humiliation all too well and was pleasant to the scurrying, worried first year men.

It started to be fun.

There was still math every term, Naval history, literature; study from 6 p.m. on, lights out at 9:55, but there were weekends, varsity athletics, required attendance at football games…

I was a second year man, a Youngster, in full dress, at Annapolis with Bancroft Hall as a background.

In my second, Youngster year, spring came, and with it, the verdant explosion of glossy white dogwood blossoms a visual decor that overwhelmed the campus…and was my nemesis. This was before the days of antihistamines, and I was wildly allergic to the pollen.

I'd had the experience in my Plebe year and once warned, twice shy, I had planned in advance the second year onslaught. I boned ahead in April for final exams, before the villain pollen saturated the air, and in May, during finals, I was in the hospital, my eyes glued shut and my nose an inflamed torrent of mucus. I put hot poultices on my eyes to open them enough that I could make it through the exams in order to survive for year three as a Second Classman.

I participated in intramural touch football which I loved until my front teeth and jaw were broken and I needed major dental repair.

I had gone home on leave after the first year and became reacquainted with the best girlfriend of Carol Rue, who had been an ex-girlfriend of mine. I chanced on Jan Paulson in Haig's Restaurant, realized how beautiful she had always been, walked her home, had a good conversation. For the next three years, while Jan was at the University of Wisconsin, when I was home, we got together for dinners, hiking, swimming, Christmas, and New

Year's. In her senior year (my Youngster year), I walked her back to her sorority dorm and was hit hard: I was in love…deeply and forever. Jan, petite, slender, with a tiny nose, and impeccably ladylike manners, was more than a friend. I wanted to be by her side for life. At Christmas, in 1952, I gave her the Naval Academy gold crest pin which I later supplemented with an engagement ring.

By my fourth year, I sent a letter invitation, a ticket, and arranged for her stay at the Astoria Hotel for the annual Army/Navy game in Philadelphia. The Midshipmen had to march into the stadium in formation, sit together (no 'drags'—dates—allowed) and march out together.

She later laughed about sitting with the other girls behind an odoriferous mascot goat, not with me. But there were parties, a breakfast, and a wonderful time.

The best times at the Academy were the summers.

In June at the end of my Plebe year, after exams, I was instructed to pack my sea bag with standard issue clothing. Three destroyers, several cruisers, and a battleship were anchored in salt water off the US Navel Academy Yard.

This was a modern armada going to Europe, an armada that rolled and bounced like tiny corks in a massive storm that roiled and tossed, churned and blew, fumed and tormented across the Atlantic from Norfolk, Virginia to Scotland.

My ship did a wild roll that threw a sailor working with me completely across the engine room into a steel bulkhead. I got help for the man and then checked the Inclinometer. It read 44 degrees. The destroyer took green water down the stacks and blew out two M-type boilers in the boiler room. No one was allowed above decks constantly awash with stormy waves. The ship was crippled.

I was one of the few who was not seasick, though green malaise and wretched vomiting were commonplace around me.

Since I was in the Engineering Department, naturally, I was assigned to chip paint!

I was elated with the newness of all the experiences:

One was induction on July 4, 1950 into the Royal Order of Blue Noses for crossing the Arctic Circle. I, along with other inductees, were paraded in skivvies on the deck and hosed down with icy water straight out of the North Sea. I had never been that blue with cold, even coming from Wisconsin!

I saw the top of Scotland, was in Bergan, Norway in port for a week, and went on liberty with a classmate, Midshipman Jim Burgess, taking a sardine boat to Hardanger Fiord to see 1,500 foot waterfalls from the glaciers and then spend several wonderful days luxuriating under goose down comforters in Ulvik at a resort hotel with an expansive deck overlooking the dark velvet blue of the waters and green of the steep hills.

We landed in Portsmouth, England at a coal dock and I went to London on leave where I was taken aback by seeing my first charwoman in a public bathroom. Unfortunately, I was standing at a urinal at the time. I was so embarrassed that I put things away much too quickly.

My uniform dry cleaned well.

From the same coal dock I watched the British Film Company shooting The Cruel Sea with the British frigate, the HMS Dorchestershire and simulated ice. Then came maneuvers off Spain and Portugal, where I could see the silhouette of ancient Lisbon but was not allowed ashore.

The end of my second year, as a Youngster, saw the Air Cruise.

I was transferred all over the U. S.—in a series of internship-like assignments—to a NAS Patuxent River where test pilots were trained for the Navy. To a SAC base in Louisiana where nuclear weapons were stored—for lectures and tours where I was coldly not welcomed by the Air Force, but where my interest in flying quickened. To a fighter base in Colorado, To NAS Cherry Point in Norfolk, Virginia. For two weeks to Little Creek, Virginia in amphibious warfare making beach landings and being a "Marine". To Texas, Love Field—NAS Dallas, the Naval Air Station

A few years later I made my first military cross country landing at Love Field in an F9-F on a runway that goes into a lake and taught me caution. I was the only one of four who did not brake so hard that a tire blew out.

One small triumph of that summer buoyed my spirits. I gave up my annual leave to be an exchange student at West Point.

I was a "kadoodler"—the best shot in the top five. The major who was part of the faculty was so angry that a Navy midshipman had bested all the Army men at machine guns and rifles—becoming a sharpshooter rifleman and an expert pistol man—that he refused to hand the trophy to me and made a lieutenant give it out.

At the end of my second year at Annapolis, I volunteered to exchange with a West Point cadet to be at Army Camp Buckner. I wanted to learn everything about small arms: M1 rifles, 30 caliber carbines, 30 caliber light machine guns, 45 caliber Colt pistols, and Browning automatic rifles. To the chagrin of Army officers, I outgunned the West Point cadets.

Some experiences were more distressing than fun.

On leave at the end of that year, I went to San Francisco to hitch a ride on a submarine to Hawaii. I had confided in my friend and roomie Joe Muka that I really wanted to be a submariner, though Joe had been urging me to learn to fly.

The submarine to Hawaii was experimenting with a new device called a snorkel to allow the Diesel engines to breathe oxygen by temporarily taking that oxygen from the living compartments when the submarine was under water which lapped over the snorkel. The unsuccessful experiment was a painful flop. My ear drums popped. I had constant earaches.

All I desired was to get back to the Academy.

Flight experience at Annapolis was in an N3-N, a single engine pontoon sea aircraft. First Class Midshipmen could apply for Flight Training and Joe Muka, my roommate, who had a private pilot's license, had been singing the joys of flying. Whether it was the carrot of friendship or the stick of the submarine, I began to contemplate, consider, and then resurrect my childhood dream of flying.

CHAPTER 6—

THE SALAD YEARS

When I learned that I needed eye surgery,
I finally knew what I wanted from life—
to fly—to be a pilot!

June, 1953. Graduation! Made it! Amen

Before graduation, after finals, each Annapolis graduate drew in a lottery a random billet number, and I, Ensign Scott, was lucky, as I so often had been and would be during the hazardous flying years ahead. With a number in the low 70's, I was given a choice of hundreds of assignments, and I chose flight training with a proviso that I would first be a "black shoe" officer with experience on a ship.

In July, 1953, for seven months, I was assigned to the U. S. S. Randolph (CVA-15). Green, just out of the Academy, but eager and willing, I was given the job as the Assistant Fire Control Officer and later as the Fire Control Officer. Reporting to me were two Warrant Officers and three Chief Petty Officers with 20 plus years of experience in Fire Control electronics.

They saved my salty butt!

The task of Fire Control is to use search radar to acquire a target. When a target is sighted by the acquisition radar (the kind that one sees on television shows), the target automatically is referred to the more exact x-band radar. It then becomes the task of the Fire Control officers to electronically aim the cannons and guns. Keep in mind that the target aircraft is traveling at great speed while the ship is pitching up, down, and sideways…to understand the complexity and importance of this task. The men apparently liked me; my superior, Commander Edwards, a "Mustang" himself, up from the ranks and close to retirement, trusted me to assignments beyond the extent of my knowledge.

Edwards gave me the task of liaison man between the Chief Gunnery Officer and the Special Weapons Unit, a team of highly trained atomic experts. I got top secret clearance to go into the bowels of the ship, through the only hatch which was under a 24 hour armed guard. I learned a lot about atomic weapons as a result. I also used my privileged status to prowl the decks and learn the launching procedures for the aircraft that constantly took off and landed, gaining knowledge that was later quite useful. All went well.

This was the time of Haitian Crisis—one of the many to come—and I was dispatched to Port au Prince as the Shore Patrol officer with a crew to quell riots. The platoon of Shore Patrol were headquartered in a beautiful hotel, the Roosevelt, which cascaded down the mountain overlooking the deep sea harbor with a beautiful pool and an inside bar serving tropical fruit drinks and rum toddies. Idyllic!

The Haitians didn't get me, but amebic dysentery did!

They found me in the junior officers' bunk room, unconscious, in my own vomit. I was comatose with a 50-50 chance of surviving. I spent most of the crisis on board in sick bay wishing I were anywhere but there!

In January of the next year, I got my wish and was assigned to Basic Flight Training in Pensacola, Florida, but in the leave between assignments, on January 31, 1954, I earned a trophy beyond all honors that the Navy could bestow—I married Jan Paulson, my sweetheart from Mt. Horeb, the breathtakingly beautiful product of a prestigious family, to be the love and light of my life. The wedding ceremony, with Lutheran minister Einer Anderson officiating, took place in the Paulson home, a magnificent structure that in later years was put on the State and National Register of Historic Places. Together, as man and wife, we honeymooned by driving to Florida where we settled in a small, neat home on 313 Gibbs Road in Pensacola.

My wife was in for culture shock.

Back in Mt. Horeb, with its Norwegian/Scotch/German populace mixture, cleanliness was truly next to Godliness, and cleanliness meant no bugs!

In the first days there, in February, when all would be pristine and frozen in Wisconsin, Jan had to learn to get used to spiders crawling up the walls, ants in the kitchen, huge water bugs that scurried across the floor every time a light came on at night, and, worst of all, giant Palmetto beetles, black and four inches long, that launched across the room in full flight, crashing against walls and furniture. It was hard to accept, but there was nothing to do but live with them.

It did help when she met our neighbors and learned that EVERYONE carried the same burden.

Even worse, when summer came—in April—was the steaming, draining heat and humidity. With a salary of only $200 a month, there seemed no way that we could afford an air conditioner. The sheets each morning were wet with perspiration. Bathing twice a day was a necessity, not an option. We wished we could pant like dogs or crawl under the house and hide away.

There was no escape from the long, turgid days.

Her beautiful wedding gifts tarnished, crumpled, and mildewed. The final blow came when one morning we opened the door to our clothes closet and found green mold on everything: shoes, uniforms, dresses, shirts, belts...even ties.

We got an air conditioner, and the days seemed to shorten.

In the meantime, I had begun my Preflight training. Again, the puckish gods of chance tossed me aloft like a boomerang. A physical examination showed a minor defect in the cornea of my right eye which could be repaired by an operation. Nothing could have filled me more with horror than that prospect. When I had been no more than five years old, my older brother Lowell had had an accident that left him almost blind. The fear in the family had imprinted itself on my mind.

Yet it was then when I accepted the necessity of the operation, that I finally knew what I truly wanted from life—to fly—to be a pilot—a bird of prey soaring high over the round blue sphere. I would do anything.

Even that.

It was a horrible experience. The doctors pulled the eye out of its socket to repair the muscles for perfect parallel vision. However, it was successful and Jan and I in May, 1955 moved to Corpus Christi, Texas, for my Advanced Flight Training.

Pensacola had been difficult for Jan. Corpus Christi was impossible. Navy housing. Wind. Dust, dust, and more dust. Blowing sand. Scorpions. Hurricanes. Rain that beat so hard against the windows that it drove water under the sill and down the wall.

In spite of the discomfort, Luck now smiled at me, as if in repayment for the ordeal behind me: I was assigned to advanced jet training which meant fighter jets and combat, and excitement, and....

Of course, afterward, I was promptly assigned, not to jet fighters, but to a propeller squadron.

CHAPTER 7—

THE ULTIMATE THRILL:
FIRST CARRIER LANDING: 1955

The ship came up to meet me.
The tail hook caught,
not just the F9F Panther jet, but also me…all of me, forever.

Like every Navy pilot, to get my wings, I had to make six carrier landings. But before that critical day, the Navy made sure that we were all prepared. That meant that I, like all the others, had to make hundreds of trial landings on Corpus Christi's runways, the land-based equivalent, denoted on the field by lines representing the exact size, shape, and placement of wires as on a carrier. Each runway used for field mirror landing practice (FMLP's) also had the same landing mirror which was located on every aircraft carrier flight deck, this for authenticity.

I had an advantage over most young pilots. As the Fire Control Officer, I'd been on the USS Randolph. And, being curious, even nosey, I'd familiarized myself with all the workings of the carriers, particularly the deck where pilots landed and took off.

When a landing jet aircraft slams down on the flight deck, the pilot always goes to full thrust in case his tail hook does not catch any of the four cables on the flight deck.

The pilot can simply make an unobstructed touch and go landing (called a "bolter"), and he is back in the air again for his next attempt to land.

If the carrier jet pilot makes the terrible mistake of pulling his throttle to idle instead of going to full thrust when his aircraft contacts the flight deck, he has no chance of survival if his tailhook does not engage an arresting gear cable. His turbojet engine requires seven to nine seconds to come back up to full thrust with enough rpm's and thrust to remain airborne.

Unfortunately, pilot and jet aircraft crash into the ocean in three to four seconds.

In the older design, if the pilot missed the wires that were meant to arrest his aircraft, his jet had to be stopped before it plowed into the pack of aircraft parked up forward. Older carriers used steel cable nets to catch such errant aircraft. The older carriers also lacked the angled deck, so the parked aircraft were dead ahead.

Thanks to the Royal Navy of Great Britain who designed the innovative angled flight deck for aircraft carriers, the Navy jet carrier pilot is back in the air in three to four seconds at full thrust—no problem.

After the British invented the angled deck, if the jet was not caught by the wires, there was no danger of wiping out parked aircraft and crew members.

The newer system had a stand-by butterfly net made of super strong nylon which could be assembled in minutes and moved to the angled deck when needed. I was familiar with both systems.

Only once did I *almost* need to use the butterfly net, when I was in an A3B returning to the USS Roosevelt for a night landing.

In that case, on an otherwise routine night landing, much to everyone's surprise, I brought the aircraft down, touched the cables—and bolted! The tail hook had not grabbed!

It was apparent that something was wrong.

On a low-level go-around, the Landing Signal Officer shined a spotlight on the tail hook. It seemed to be in place!

I tried again. Again I bolted.

The landing signal officer told the Air Boss I was landing in the wires with an apparently functioning tail hook point.

But again I bolted. And again! And again!

In the Ready Room, pilots watched and listened. I was known for not bolting!

On deck, they realized something had to be wrong with my tail hook and they began to hurriedly assemble the butterfly net on the axial deck with the intention of pulling it over to the angled deck.

I bolted seven times and remained in the landing pattern.

With increasing apprehension, I watched my fuel supply. I had only

The AD-6 had great potential as a light attack aircraft. Its basic weight was 8 tons, yet it could carry another 8 tons of ordnance when fully loaded. This picture shows the aircraft tail hook catching an arresting gear cable.

enough fuel for a maximum of two more go-rounds!

On the eighth landing attempt—by sheer luck—the hook point aligned with the hook shaft, and I landed safely

What they found upon examination of my aircraft was that the hook point retention bolt had come loose, permitting the tail hook point to rotate on the hook shaft.

My reputation as a non-bolter remained intact. It was a mechanical failure, not my airmanship. I have to say, it was also a full measure of good luck that on that eighth try, the hook point aligned. I might have lost more than my reputation!

Again, part skill; much luck.

I had the further advantage of understanding how essential it was that the skipper keep absolute control of the speed and the position of the carrier.

Normally, the skipper tries to establish 30 knots of wind over the flight deck. This means in essence that the aircraft when landing flies 30 knots slower relative to the flight deck and arresting gear. This allows the pilot more reaction time just before flight deck touchdown. As he attempts an arrested landing, he has a better opportunity to land on the arresting gear and catch a cable with his aircraft tail hook. With 5 knots of wind, the skipper needs to order 25 knots of speed and more to allow for the flow of wind on the angled deck.

I was always quite happy to accept that advantage in every carrier landing I made.

I made first my six required carrier landings on the U. S. S. Monterey in the Gulf of Mexico in 1954 in an antiquated SNJ, a propeller aircraft with a metal skin.

Later, after taking off from Corpus Christi for Pensacola, we were briefed and sent out without an instructor and made six jet carrier landings. Both sets of landings were fun and required care and attention, but it was not until later when I made my first solo jet landing that I learned why carrier pilots came back and exulted in the shower like over-hyped teenagers.

My first solo carrier jet landing was in an F9F Panther.
The carrier was a bright sunlit punctuation dot in the ocean.
I lined up my aircraft for the landing, mind at ready, pulse elevated!
The ship grew exponentially!
It rushed up toward me at 100 miles an hour, as if it intended to smash into my face.
Beyond the angled deck lay the vast expanse of endless ocean. The wires were invisible, but from experience, I knew they were there. Something—like a fist—twisted my gut.
My hand clutched the stick.
All or nothing. Here I come!
The ship came inexorably up to meet me.
What if I didn't make it!
The instant my aircraft landing gear slammed into the flight deck, I pushed the throttle to full thrust. Then my tail hook grabbed a wire. The shoulder straps tugged at my chest. My aircraft stopped cold.
I had done it! Glory be!!!
I laughed in a triumphant shout but the tears streamed down my face.
That tail hook caught the landing arresting cable—not just the jet, but me…forever.
I knew that this was what I was born to do. My future was ordained that wonderful day in 1955.

In Naval aviation, the saying goes that landing a jet at night on a carrier is the only time a pilot can have a bowel movement and an orgasm simultaneously. Well, that may be a bit exaggerated, but it isn't far from fact.

I never tired of landing my jet on a carrier. Every landing was a thrill, equal to that first one, or better.

CHAPTER 8—

ATOMIC DELIVERY: 1956 DEPLOYMENT ON THE YORKTOWN:

My job was to practice carrier landings
They called it duty but I knew better.
It was sheer joy.

In Oct. 11, 1955, I, now Lt. jg. R. Scott Beat, received my coveted Naval Aviation wings of gold. Naval Aviator Number V-8116 for life.

We moved from Corpus Christi Naval Air Station to Sunnyvale, California, where I was assigned to VA-195, my first Navy squadron. This squadron was an integral part of Air Wing 19, attached to NAS, Moffett Field, California. We were to live nearby for the next four years, from 1955 to 1958.

My operational flying adventures of my Navy career would then begin in earnest.

The VA-195 had originally been Attack Squadron TWENTY ABLE. They were called the Dambusters because on May 2, 1951 during the Korean War, the Skyraiders made precision low level runs and delivered aerial torpedoes to destroy the Hwa Chon Dam in North Korea. The destruction of the dam had been unsuccessfully attempted by the Air Force and by Navy bombers, so it was an important accomplishment. They were then flying the AD-1 Skyraider.

They transitioned from the propeller driven Skyraiders, known as Spads, to the jet powered A-4 Skyhawk in July 1959, after I left the squadron.

By 1964, when the Vietnam crisis had deepened, the Dambusters made their fourth consecutive deployment on the USS Bon Homme Richard with the Seventh Fleet. Our squadron logged more combat flight hours and sorties than any other squadron in Air Wing Nineteen.

We called the A-4 a Tinkertoy because it had only two hours of fuel.

At this point in my career I was deployed on the USS Yorktown (CVA 10) as an Atomic Delivery pilot about to launch on my flight in the AD-6 Skyraider. I made more than 100 arrested landings to become a Centurion on the Yorktown.

During my first year at Moffett Field, I was among the new, less experienced pilots who practiced carrier landings often in anticipation of inevitable future squadron deployments overseas when we would be assigned for six to eight months or longer on an aircraft carrier.

On land, my job was to practice carrier landings at Field Mirror Landing Practice, FMLP.

An FMLP is an area exactly equivalent to the landing area on an aircraft carrier. The pattern was painted on the runway and each pilot was expected to land again and again until it was habit and routine. When a pilot missed the painted wires—which on the carrier would catch the aircraft—it was called a "bolter" and the man who missed became the butt of the jokes for the day.

Twenty, 30, 40, 50, 100 landings. The practice never seemed to end, but it was vital.

The Navy carrier pilot who did not excel for lack of practice or inattention might crash on the flight deck or into the ocean and be killed—a severe and forbidding reminder as to why practice landings were never to be approached with a cavalier attitude.

I put in between 200 and 250 flight hours, invaluable experience that was soon to save my life.

Other pilot training always in progress in VA-195 was simulated long-range, low level atomic weapons delivery on selected fictitious enemy targets. It was not unusual to make training flights between eight to nine and one half hours duration, always with a coastal penetration at "extreme" minimum altitudes to avoid simulated enemy radar discovery.

Most of the carrier flight decks I was to land on in the 1960's and '70's, were approximately 70 feet above the ocean—which allowed little room for inattention even after flying for five hours or more while wearing a rubber life-saving vest in a cockpit with no air conditioning at temperatures over 100 degrees Fahrenheit.

(Not to worry, however! I would have exactly one quart of water in a canteen to last for the entire flight!)

Each briefing for each low-level flight would begin: "Immediately after your catapult launch, descend to cruising altitude!!!" (That didn't take long.)

The first of my many aircraft carrier deployments was eight months in the Western Pacific aboard the USS Yorktown (CVA-10) in 1957. My air wing was the first to use the newly installed canted, or angled, deck on the Yorktown, that saved many an incoming pilot from disaster.

Every aircraft carrier, before going out to sea, must go through an ORI, an Operational Readiness Inspection.

We were off Hawaii, and it was simulated that four submarines were taking pot shots at us. Men were on duty for 48 hours at a stretch.

They would announce: "You had a hit, so the air conditioning is out of order."

Temperatures rose to 110 degrees. Though it was only a practice, the air conditioning was not restarted.

We were to learn to live with the worst that could happen.

Meals were incidental. Sleep did not exist. It was part of the Navy training.

Oh, yes, the Navy prepared men! You'd better believe it!

CHAPTER 9—

THE BIRDS AND I: 1956

*I had the limited experience of several hundred hours
of pilot time in AD-6 aircraft and approximately 100 landings
on carrier simulated runways in mostly clear weather.
I naively felt certain that I was well qualified for anything.*

It was 4:30 a.m. when my alarm clock shrilled, irritating and abrasive. That was its saving grace; it always awakened me; I never could sleep through that noise.

I had rolled out of my warm cocoon in the master bedroom of my home in Sunnyvale, California, and careful not to awaken my sweet wife, I shuffled off to the kitchen to brew some life sustaining coffee. I completed my bathroom activities as I swallowed the dregs of my second cup of java. Then, quickly donning my uniform, I fumbled through my pockets for my car keys.

There was no chance of forcing down a breakfast at such an early hour. I unplugged the coffee maker and turned off the lights; I snatched a banana and an apple from the kitchen table for a delayed breakfast later in the morning.

The predawn morning had an autumnal chill which reminded me to zip up my leather flight jacket. I unlocked the car and strapped myself in. It was time to begin my predawn commute to NAS Moffett Field, California. A thoroughly normal morning.

I was young, full of myself, cocky, sure…and untested. I had no inkling of the near tragedy the day would bring.

A smile involuntarily marched across my face as I crossed the usually busy road, El Camino Real. It was too early for much traffic, but I was reminded of a favorite Squadron saying, "If you can escape crashing and burning during the morning commute to the airfield, the dangerous part of the day is done!" Nevertheless, I was mildly surprised at completing the commute in one half the time it would take three harrowing hours later.

I entered the squadron building where the flight briefing was scheduled as Jerry Mack arrived. Our early morning greetings were more like sleepy grunts than cheerful salutations. After a wake-up cup of hot java, we tried another, more cordial, "Good morning."

Jerry was a handsome 24 year old pilot with dark brown curly hair and a smile that, on occasion, totally defrosted the aloofness of young damsels at the Officers Club bar. Not a braggart, he often wore a wide grin when accused of seldom sleeping in his own bed. His sobriety was never in doubt; his skills were honed. That is all I needed and wanted to know about him.

It was 5:20 a.m. as we entered the squadron ready room at Moffett Field in California for the 5:30 a.m. pilots' briefings on the day's training flights.

This cool October morning in 1956, I, LT. (jg) Beat and my wing man, LT (jg) Jerry Mack, would simulate launching as a two aircraft section of AD-6 atomic delivery attack aircraft from a fictitious United States Navy aircraft carrier located at position "Alpha" in the Pacific Ocean.

The aircraft was a beauty—the Douglas Skyraider with a single reciprocating engine and a four bladed propeller. It had a basic weight of 16,000 pounds and carried 16,000 pounds of ordinance when fully loaded.

Some eight hours after takeoff, we would recover aboard the fictitious aircraft carrier (NAS Moffett Field) following our simulated atomic delivery on our designated enemy target (in this case, Bakersfield, California).Our flight would take us low level over the Pacific, north to the coast of Oregon where we would make an extremely low-level coastal entry to avoid radar detection. We would remain at low level away from populated areas to avoid interception by simulated enemy fighters; we'd proceed generally south over mountainous terrain past Bryce Canyon, the northern part of Grand Canyon; then west over desert terrain to Bakersfield, where we would simulate the launching of an atomic weapon.

We two Navy pilots would simulate and carry out a long range, low level atomic delivery mission without landing or refueling for eight hours.

It would begin when we started our engines.

Training flights such as ours had a much deeper and more serious purpose than a flat-hatting joy ride. We had to arrive at many geographic check points on course, on time, on altitude. Every simulation, every radio call, every aerial maneuver was designed to hone us into proficient atomic attack pilots for the dreaded point in the future when all the games were over and when our lives could be in grave combat peril.

Jerry and I had relatively little experience, but military aviators as a group are a vain, cocksure bunch who truly believe they can make aircraft perform incredible feats in flight.

The carefully orchestrated training sorties were designed to inhibit our overconfidence and replace it with better judgment, proficiency and logic. All pilots become better aviators with more flight experience, and, although we had no notion of it, we were due that October day to learn a humbling lesson.

In truth, we both had the limited experience of several hundred hours of pilot time in AD-6 aircraft and approximately 100 landings on land based runways in mostly clear weather. We naively felt certain that we were well qualified in spite of our modest level of flight experience.

It is said that "You can always tell a military pilot, but you can't tell him much."

That is particularly true of pilots with between 500 and 1000 hours of flight experience. The grim reality of fatal accidents by pilots with such minimal experience levels is sadly and shockingly reflected in military aviation statistics and aircraft accident records.

There was absolutely nothing exciting or romantic about our predawn verbal rehearsal and briefing concerning our mission. Squadron missions, conducted by a schooled air intelligence officer, covered air routes, navigation check points, en route weather, emergency procedures, restricted or prohibited air space, navigational aids en route, radio use and frequencies, alternate routes to targets if required, review of charts, maps and photographs, checks for personal survival gear, and NOTAMS (notices to airmen—updated hazards, restrictions and possible en route difficulties to be aware of).

We strutted out of the briefing like two immature peacocks, the boring part of our mission complete. An easy day! We knew it all.

Unbeknown to us, we soon would experience and relearn that not everything happens as planned—especially with military flight.

The eastern sky was beginning to illuminate as we completed our pre-takeoff check lists at the end of the active runway. All our flight and engine instruments told us we were ready to launch. Since I had more seniority, I—who five minutes before had been a strutting flyboy—was the section leader and now strongly felt the serious responsibility.

I keyed my radio transmitter. "Moffett Tower, Chippy 6731 ready for takeoff; section of 2."

"Roger, Chippy 6731, section of two cleared for takeoff. Immediately after takeoff, turn left to a heading of 270 degrees and climb to and maintain 5, 500 feet until feet wet. Then cleared to en route frequency. Good flight, Sirs,"

"Wilco, Moffett Tower. Thank you."

All routine. So smooth. I was in charge. Had done my job. All was right with the world.

We quickly rendezvoused after take off as we turned westward toward the Santa Rosa Mountains. We crossed the mountain range and commenced a slow descent toward the calm surface of the Pacific Ocean as daylight began to increase our visibility and depth perception. We leveled off at 100 feet above the ocean and established our magnetic heading based on airspeed and surface wind velocity.

In short order, we were cruising at 100 feet and had enough daylight now to descend to our cruising altitude of 50 feet above sea level, a training practice to avoid enemy radar tracking and intercept. We settled into our flight with a thorough in-flight check list and careful scan of each instrument in every row of the instrument panels in our respective cockpits; everything was completely normal.

We cruised northward at 50 feet above the ocean surface past the Farallon Islands west of San Francisco Bay. Visibility continued to improve as the early morning sun effectively forced the reluctant fog and haze seaward and offshore.

An immense gaggle of seagulls and other marine birds busily searched and scavenged food from an ebbing tide flowing out of San Francisco Bay. The birds were highly agitated and complained vociferously about our infringing on their low altitude food searching air space.

I hand signaled my wing man to climb so we could reduce the probability of bird strike damage to our aircraft. We had just commenced a slow climb when, out of the morning mist, we encountered a dozen or more seagulls frantically trying to avoid our aircraft.

One or more gulls passed through my propeller arc. There was an explosion as feathers and bird parts passed my cockpit at 175 miles an hour.

"Wow! Jerry, did you get hit?"

"Don't think so," he responded.

"Let's climb to 5,000 feet toward San Francisco and do a check."

"Roger."

Since I had the most obvious bird strikes, Jerry visually inspected my aircraft first. He flew close, checked for oil leaks, dents, damaged radio antenna or pitot tube and gave a "thumbs up." I returned the favor. No significant problems. We both inhaled a deep sigh of relief. Before turning back to intercept our planned flight track, I ordered a careful check of all instruments as further assurance that all was well.

As I scanned every instrument on my instrument panel, I noted that we were 66 nautical miles northwest of the San Francisco Tacan transmitter.

Before I could finish my instrument check, "up jumped the devil!"

My engine cylinder head temperature was climbing and approaching the overheat red line on the gauge. I opened my cowl flaps full to circulate maximum cooling air inside the engine cowling and continued the climb to 5,000 feet.

Jerry read my mind like an open book and flew a tight formation on my aircraft, visually checking for damage—before I had time to ask. He was my kind of pilot, one who thought ahead and invariably took the safest and best action.

"My engine cylinder head temp is red line and climbing."

I may have sounded calm, but I was sweating and tense.

"I'll try to coax this sick bird to NAS Alameda before I have a total failure. Radio NAS Alameda with our position off the SFO Tacan and request an emergency straight-in approach to landing with no wave off! Ask Alameda to alert sea air rescue with our position."

"Wilco, Scott. Squawking "Emergency" on my IFF and calling Alameda Tower now," he replied.

"I plan to ride my aircraft down to a water ditching if my engine quits before I'm feet dry. Give the SAR an accurate Tacan fix on my crash. If I bail out, those offshore winds will carry me more miles out to sea and more minutes from the SAR team."

I did not want the rescue units to have any extra miles to reach me—miles that meant extra minutes in the cold, rough ocean that might tip the scales the wrong way. An extra ten miles closer to land could make the difference in surviving or not. I was intensely aware of the choppy, cold salt water that waited for me some 4,000 feet below: I knew by observing the ocean waves and the way the white caps were falling back into the wave troughs that winds were blowing seaward at 20 to 25 knots.

I was no longer the cocky, sassy know-it-all or even the responsible section leader. I was a scared kid! In an aircraft on the way to imminent death in a choppy sea!

I asked for divine guidance as I continued to reluctantly trade off some of my precious altitude for reduced power settings to lower the engine overheat temperature.

I could see some scorched paint on my engine cowling and tried to recall if the paint was like that when we took off.

I gently pulled back my throttle, lowering the engine manifold pressure a bit more. My engine backfired like a cannon; a black cloud of smoke exploded from the cowling. I swallowed my heart and quickly pushed the fuel mixture to "full rich." That was no time to have an engine sputter or quit! Nor did I want any of the nearly red hot cylinder heads on my radial engine to fail.

"Whoops!" Jerry exclaimed on the radio. "Do you still have power?"

"Yes, but I don't know for how long." I'm sure he could hear the fear in my voice. It was certainly there."

The San Francisco Golden Gate Bridge was in sight, but it seemed 100 miles away instead of the actual 25 miles in slightly reduced visibility. I felt I could wait to reduce power even more and continue my power glide. I was between a rock and a hard place, as that icy water mocked me and beckoned some 2,500 feet below.

We overflew the Golden Gate Bridge at 1,800 feet. My spirits began to improve as I saw my emergency airfield across the Bay. It seemed at that moment that I had a good chance of making the runway—barring a complete engine failure.

Less than five minutes left to put that sick bird on the runway!

"Dear God, please don't let me down at this point," became an unspoken refrain.

Alameda Control Tower had earlier cleared me for a straight-in approach and landing. They cautioned me that my wheels were still up when I was one mile from the runway. I opened my cockpit canopy as I acknowledged the tower warning and told them I would lower my landing gear when I was very close in. It was likely that the large increase of drag from lowering the landing gear early would require more power than my hot engine could produce, and it might fail before I reached the runway.

The fire trucks and crash vehicles were all in position alongside the runway.

No forgiveness for errors—things would happen very quickly now. Five hundred yards to the runway threshold—no wave off this time!

Over the threshold at 40 feet—full propeller RPM—landing gear down—half flaps down—throttle to idle. I touched down on the runway centerline as my engine failed and the propeller screeched loudly to an instant halt!

"Thank you, Lord, for letting me help you put this aircraft on the runway!"

"Alameda Tower, I may need a tow to the parking area. Thank you for your help."

Roger, Sir. A tow tractor is on the way. Great landing, Sir"

"Thank you, Tower. Piece of cake."

Thank goodness they could not see my knees knocking and the sweat pouring off my face or feel the pounding of my heart!

At the parking ramp, an inspection revealed half a large seagull with wing outstretched and feathers covering most of the cooling fins in the entrance to my engine oil cooler.

Just that simple—just that unpredictable—just that vulnerable.

Some pilots will tell you that flying is all skill and no luck. Wrong! It is a delicate balance that permits survival. The Navy had furnished the homework; I had contributed the skill; Another had generously supplied the luck.

CHAPTER 10—

LIFE WITH THE A3B

Had it been a real run, a real bomb, a real disaster to mankind,
all those aboard would have been like the crisp, charred bits
of World Trade paper floating toward the depths of angry Neptune.

My first deployment off the USS Roosevelt after my wife and I had moved to Sanford, Florida, was an interesting one—in retrospect a life-threatening one—but at the time, it was merely another assignment, simply a part of the routine of flying with the Navy.

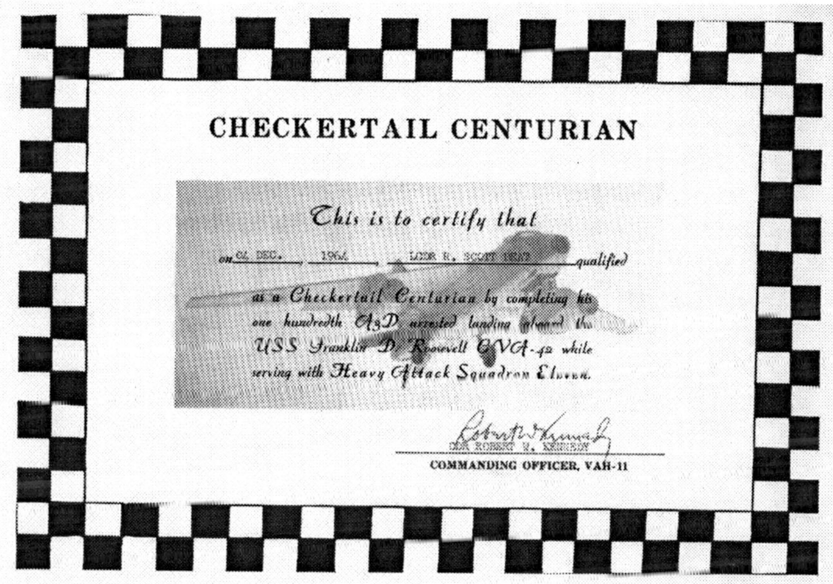

Of my almost 1000 arrested landings, I made more than 200 on the USS
Franklin D. Roosevelt, (CVA 42) while attached to the Heavy Attack
Squadron Eleven. I was awarded this certificate as proof of the
accomplishment

Like the entire VAH-11 squadron to which I had been assigned, I was charged with the delivery of nuclear weapons. Such a simple way to disguise the potential destruction of the earth!

What it meant in actuality for the pilots and the crews, was endless, interminable, mind and body numbing practice runs, each with the goal of delivering a hydrogen bomb to an exact target.

A bomb that could eviscerate our world.

The daily routine was something like this: We would be briefed by the Air Intelligence Officer in the Squadron Ready Room as to the target for the run. As the pilot, I would hasten to my A-3B, its swept back wings a race horse with flattened ears twitching for the excitement to begin. I'd scramble aboard, strap myself in, go through the pre-start check list:

"Throttle off, proper circuit breakers in, fuel check…"

The aircraft captain was on the flight deck. The huffer blew compressed air into the engine turbine to get the engine up to starting speed. When it reached starting RPM with the throttle off to prevent fuel from entering the engine prematurely, I would hit the engine starter igniter switch and simultaneously put the engine throttle in idle. The engine stabilized at idle speed, consuming 500 pounds of jet fuel per hour while at idle. The aircraft captain would connect the huffer to the second engine and the starting procedure was repeated.

After the aircraft was attached to the catapult, the flight deck catapult officer would signal me to go to full thrust. As soon as I had checked all engine instruments for "Go," I would salute the catapult officer located on the flight deck by the aircraft port wingtip. The catapult officer then would touch the flight deck with his hand held wand and one second later, the deck edge operator fired the catapult.

In two seconds, my aircrew and I in our 39 1/2 ton stallion would be accelerated to approximately 150 miles per hour—depending on gross takeoff weight—in 200 feet down the catapult!

Out of the starting gate, my sleek gray stallion would leap over the sun bright Mediterranean lapping below, unaware of the war games that could have easily made the quiet sea a maelstrom of human fire and destruction. At the instructions of the bombardier, I would turn the aircraft toward the target—always over land.

The A3B with its celebrated "Checkertail" motif was used for Heavy Attack to carry nuclear bombs. It was not suitable for electronic spying, since it could only accommodate three people, but because it carried a tremendous amount of fuel, it became a tanker. I flew it in both configurations.

Meanwhile, on the ground below, the technicians tracked the progress of my aircraft.

The bombardier, who was actually the vital person on the run, took control as we neared the target.

It was "Left two degrees. Good. Steady. Steady."

I became a tool, a willing robot, responding mechanically to commands, instantaneously moving the yoke to another's shouted commands, my quick responses vital to the mission.

"Steady. Right one degree"

There was no "Yes, Sir," no salutes, only instantaneous reaction, as if I were a computer controlled puppet.

Ten seconds before the drop, the bombardier opened the bomb bay doors.

"Opening! Bomb bay!"

The change in the aerodynamic contour of the aircraft meant I needed to quickly increase engine thrust and readjust aircraft trim at that critical moment.

"Bombs away! Bomb bay doors shut!"

An ultra high frequency beep—triggered when the bombardier pressed the bomb release button—would sound, not long, but shrill, an announcement of the probable doom of hundreds of thousands of unsuspecting human beings below—eating, talking, arguing, selling, buying, negotiating, loving—simply living.

The bombardier would press the release button that in an actual world would allow an H bomb to annihilate buildings, trees, vehicles…and people.

At that moment I again became the controlling force. I added full thrust, pushed both throttles to full forward so the aircraft shot straight line, fast out of there—in the vain hope that my stallion could outrun the red-black hell that would boil up from the impact, the roaring winds of a demonic world that burst into a mushroom cloud never before seen.

I was again a six year old, back in the woods behind my Mt. Horeb house where the bad guys always lost and the good ones came home triumphant.

The difference was enormous: Had it been a real run, a real bomb, a real disaster to mankind, I—and all those aboard—would have been like the crisp, charred bits of World Trade paper floating toward the depths of angry Neptune.

But the actual bomb was never dropped.

I would fly my tired charger back to its stall, go through debriefing and the next day, repeat the training runs, always hoping that they would remain just that—

CHAPTER 11—

APRIL, 1958
THE BON HOMME RICHARD

A dead stick landing on a dark black night
on a rain swept carrier with a pitching deck Is unheard of.
But it happened.

The skipper of any aircraft carrier assumes a mind-boggling set of responsibilities, and on one particular day in April, 1958, Captain David McCampbell, U. S. Navy, the skipper of the USS Bon Homme Richard (CVA-31), would tap all his measured experience and knowledge.

I, too, was to be required to measure all my skills before flight operations that evening were completed, but in a different, more immediate, way.

The ship had spent a long day of flight operations beginning at 0700 hours, moving in and out of moderate to intense rain squalls.

The predicament that the Bon Homme Richard's commanding officer had was that the winds over the South China Sea during flight operations were blowing southward out of nearby China's mainland. This meant that whenever the ship was recovering or launching aircraft, the carrier and the two accompanying destroyer escorts had to steam at substantial speed directly toward the coast of China and toward a significant amount of maritime traffic just off the Chinese coast.

This was, of course, necessary to allow landing aircraft to land at a safe airspeed.

The same wind requirements are needed for aircraft during takeoff from the carrier deck. Wind down the flight deck allowed slower catapult end-speeds to launch aircraft into the air at safe, minimum flying speeds, For this, the carrier skipper needed to head in toward the Chinese mainland during all landings and take offs.

Then, because of the unfavorable winds, the carrier division was required to turn around and steam downwind away from the Chinese coast to build up that needed distance and prepare for the next aircraft launch/recovery cycle.

That day the sea was choppy with 10 to 20 foot waves and winds sometimes gusting to 20 knots. These weather conditions caused the carrier and its 889 foot flight deck to noticeably roll, pitch, and sometimes yaw, making aircraft recovery even more difficult and time-consuming.

Another more subtle, but critical concern for the skipper, was the ship's fuel consumption. Fuel consumption increased geometrically the faster he had to steam. The ship had eight ravenous boilers that each gulped thousands of pounds of fuel per hour to operate the four main engines that, with super heated steam, drove the turbines. Each main engine could produce 62,500 horsepower, if required, This, of course, pales in contrast to today's nuclear powered carriers, but at the time, the skipper had to factor in refueling his destroyer escorts underway from the carrier's own supply of NSFO (Navy Standard Fuel Oil).

The skipper was always aware that a division of U. S. warships steaming unannounced into Chinese territorial waters east of Hong Kong at any speed could create an international incident or crisis—not a wise political maneuver to promote world peace!

I had had only one carrier flight on that rain-swept April afternoon, and I was scheduled to fly again that night.

Little did I anticipate what lay ahead of me.

Darkness crept over the ship—muffled, overcast darkness devoid of moonlight or starlight.

Black nothingness at the end of the ship.

The only plus was that the squall line retreated and relented somewhat with the setting sun which made the flight deck slightly more stable than had been the case during the daylight arrested landings.

The steadier, more stable flight deck with less pitching and rolling was a welcome relief.

Afternoon flight operations had been completed two hours before sunset to allow the carrier division to steam an additional 50 nautical miles southward, away from China and offshore shipping traffic to assure that no minor navigation errors during night flight operations would precipitate a crisis with the Chinese government.

We finished our preflight briefings in the VA-195 ready room.

The intercom crackled out, "Pilots, man your aircraft."

I became a Centurion on this ship with nearly 100 arrested landings. The Bon Homme Richard, (CVA-31). a 27,100 ton Essex class aircraft carrier, was my home for two extended deployments in the Pacific during which I was an atomic delivery pilot. The ship came to be familiarly known as the "Bony Dick,"—as long as the commanding officer didn't hear of it!

I arrived on the flight deck and did my preflight inspection by the dim red glow of my flashlight. (No white lights are allowed during night flight operations because it could ruin night vision.) My aircraft captain helped me strap myself into the cockpit while he briefed me on the physical condition of my bird as he knew it to be.

Jenks' last comment was, "Man, it's pitch black out there tonight!"

I wasn't amused and snapped, "Thanks! You really know how to reassure your pilot! Now get off my wing! I have places to go and things to do!"

The carrier division commander, Rear Admiral William Scheoch, was always pleased to find "mildly adverse" conditions to provide excellent readiness training for future combat. He was correct, but it was seldom neither safe nor comfortable gaining that experience.

He would certainly have been happy that dark evening!

A few minutes before 2000 hours (8 p.m.), I taxied forward for my turn on the starboard (right) catapult. I had just finished my pre-takeoff check list, and my aircraft was "Go."

Soon my "bird" would be attached to the catapult. The Catapult Officer would appear near the port (left) wing tip along the wing's leading edge. In the night, he would raise his green, illumined wand above his head, and with that vertical wand, he would start a circular motion signaling me to go to full power; I would make a quick, last-second scan of my engine instruments at full power. If all was normal, I would signal "go" to the Catapult Officer by turning on my wing tip lights. The Catapult Officer then would swing his overhead green wand in a downward arc, touching the flight deck with the wand.

One second later the deck edge catapult operator would fire the catapult.

Pilot and aircraft, from a dead stop, accelerate to flying speed in 200 feet, and in less than three seconds are airborne at about 150 miles per hour (depending on the take off gross weight).

The Bon Homme Richard was equipped with hydraulic powered catapults that had a terrific initial acceleration peak at the beginning of the catapult stroke.

It always made me imagine that I had just been hit across the back of my armored pilot's seat with a high speed telephone pole used like a baseball bat.

As soon as possible, I as the pilot must focus my eyes on the flight instruments to ascertain that the aircraft is right side up, wings level, accelerating, and climbing. Anything less can violently shorten flight time and life span.

All this accomplished, I searched ahead in the expanse of darkness to locate the aircraft lights of my section leader, and I immediately rendezvoused with his aircraft.

Our mission for our night sortie was to proceed 105 nautical miles outbound on the 210 magnetic radial of the carrier and report positions of all sea borne traffic relative to "home plate" (our carrier). That would be boring and easy enough.

"Bulgie" Solomon, my section leader and former neighbor, and I were together on our second extended Western Pacific carrier cruise. Our previous cruise was aboard the USS Yorktown (CVA-10) for a period of seven plus months during 1956–57. We had mutually enjoyed a number of flight experiences and well knew each other's thinking and routines while airborne. We were comfortable with and had faith in each other's judgment. He was two or more years senior to me and had many hundreds of pilot hours of flight experience more than I.

Bulgie was a constantly smiling, self-confident guy with a great sense of humor who gracefully deflected barbs fired his way about his insipient corpulence without losing his composure. As a proficient Landing Signal Officer (LSO) he had saved several pilots from grave mishaps during their carrier landings.

We were approximately 50 nautical miles out en route to our first turn around on the 210 radial when Bulgie called for our first routine in-flight check. I meticulously checked each instrument and gauge on my instrument panel. Whenever I made such a check, I was very careful to analyze each instrument with the attitude that I would find at least one discrepancy. That seldom happened.

However, I felt it was insurance that complacency would not lull me into making an erroneous observation about what each gauge was indicating. It was my personal belief that I was less likely to make a stupid error because of monotony, fatigue, familiarity, or a moment of distraction.

I could recall when that routine of double-checking instrument readings and confirming or disproving the validity had averted a few airborne emergencies.

Paradoxically, this was perennially a pilot's game—boredom and monotony—occasionally punctuated with moments of high stress and perilous risk.

I breathed a sigh of relief upon completion of my cautious flight check as I reported the results to my section leader. All was normal—no serious discrepancies to report on that darkly threatening, rain-punctuated April night.

As a matter of routine, I did mention to Bulgie that I had experienced what I thought was occasional backfiring of my engine without any apparent engine instrument indications. I stated that I had moved my fuel mixture to "full rich" which seemed to reduce the engine backfire significantly.

"Keep a sharp eye on your engine gauges for any abnormal readings," Bulgie instructed, "and notify me if anything develops."

I reassured myself by doing an additional, precautionary fuel check that I had more than enough extra 115–145 high octane fuel in rich mixture so I would not be concerned about low fuel state prior to landing.

We continued outbound from the carrier toward our turnaround point. No surface contacts were visually sighted on our outbound leg, no faint glimmered outlines in the dark void below us. Surface conditions on the water that night probably precluded most ocean going ships from navigating outside normally traveled shipping lanes in that part of the South China Sea.

We were scheduled to complete two "out and back" round trips on our assigned 210 search radial before our recovery aboard the Bon Homme Richard.

We had completed our course reversal for our first return leg toward the carrier, when within minutes our routine flight started to unravel.

"My engine oil pressure is gradually decreasing," I reported to Bulgie, "and my engine cylinder head temperature is beginning to rise."

I'll never forget his response.

"Oh, shit!" he said.

We both knew at once what trouble I was in. I requested Bulgie to radio the carrier to apprise Air Operations of my predicament, and to request no delay in my recovery aboard ship.

My thoughts flashed back to a previous engine overheat emergency when a gull had blocked the air intake to my engine oil cooler near the Farrallon Islands in 1956.

I opened my engine cowl flaps full for maximum air cooling of my hot engine. Lessons learned from the 1956 near-disaster continued to rush forward and flood my mind with possible options:

1.) Do not reduce propeller RPM significantly or the overheating, oil-starved engine may seize.
2.) Keep the cowl flaps wide open for engine cooling.
3.) Save every foot of altitude available until your approach and landing.
4.) Maintain full rich fuel mixture.
5.) IFF to "EMERGENCY" for positive radar I.D.
6.) Let the wing man do all communicating—you're too occupied!
7.) Stay calm—ask the "Big Guy" for divine assistance—to use all the good help you can get!

Deep inside me, I mustered up all the courage I had.

I was only too aware what my survival chances were if the engine failed. It meant crashing into that angry sea with 15 foot waves in total, pitch-black darkness.

The carrier had turned into the wind for my recovery. Bulgie maneuvered our two aircraft section to align our flight path with the ship's course as Air Operations reported the carrier's course and wind over the deck.

Bulgie reminded me that when we were ordered to switch radio channels to the carrier's landing channel that if I couldn't make contact, I should go directly to guard (emergency frequency) and stay on it until I landed.

The lights of the Bon Homme Richard came into view at four miles through marginal visibility in light rain. Air Operations cleared me for a straight in approach. It was now "Show Time!"

There would be no wave-off nor a second chance with that overheated engine!

One half mile out. Landing gear down. Full flaps down. Tail hook down. Full propeller RPM. Fuel mixture rich. Cockpit canopy open. Landing check list complete."

My eyes were locked on the "meatball" on the landing signal mirror.

All aircraft carriers that recover conventional fixed wing aircraft have a gyro-stabilized elliptical shaped landing signal mirror mounted near the carrier's stern along side the flight deck edge on the port side of the ship. Further astern, a high intensity, white spotlight is adjusted to shine into the signal mirror which faces aft toward the rear of the carrier. The mirror has a horizontal row of green lights that form an apparent green line across the middle of the mirror's face. When all these elements are engineered and precisely adjusted, the landing signal mirror reflects a spot of white light on the mirror and behind the carrier at the exact angle of a perfect glide slope.

At a half mile out, the white ball of light—the meatball—appears. When the pilot adjusts his power or thrust setting to change his aircraft's rate of descent and the meatball is in the middle of the mirror on the horizontal green line, his aircraft is exactly on the glide slope, neither too high nor too low, descending at the exact speed needed to land in the arresting wires and stop on the flight deck.

I resolved minutes before that I would "fly" that meatball dead center on the glide slope without error as long as that overheated engine kept backfiring and running.

It was my only chance to survive.

As I flew over the fan tail—the stern—of the carrier, the Landing Signal Officer signaled "CUT"—power to idle.

I quickly pulled my throttle to idle, and I heard that same sickening metallic screech I heard two years before.

The engine seized!

The pilot and all eight tons of stricken aircraft with the dead engine glided the last 10 to 15 feet down and slammed into the arresting gear on the flight deck at nearly 100 miles per hour!

Dear God, what a marvelous thrill to feel my tail hook catch that arresting cable and tug aircraft and pilot to a full stop on the flight deck!

"My Gawd!" I had just made a dead stick arrested landing on an aircraft carrier at night in poor visibility with rain!! I was stunned at the improbability of such a rare event!

The flight deck crew hurriedly attached a tow tractor and towed me onto the deck edge elevator. I was lowered to the hanger deck, and just as quickly, the elevator was raised to the flight deck as the next landing aircraft engaged the arresting gear seconds later. Split second timing! Flight deck crews operated with skill, dedication, and precision. The ship and crew had demonstrated readiness for combat!

The ensuing inspection showed that an oil leak had developed in flight, and the engine was badly oil starved, which caused the overheat problem.

Later, in the squadron ready room, the Landing Signal Officer stopped by.

He smiled broadly, shook his head in wonder, and looked me directly in my eyes.

"Scott Beat, tonight you are the luckiest pilot alive! When your engine seized and you dead stick glided past the LSO platform, those engine exhaust stacks glowed visibly red. I thought you were a goner, you S.O.B. Congratulations!"

I was grinning from ear to ear. "Thanks!" I responded.

Skill and luck once again! I thanked Bulgie for his experienced guidance and backup.

No. I didn't forget divine assistance, either. I thanked Him/Her profusely before I could get to sleep somewhere on the South China Sea one rainy, overcast night in April, 1958.

CHAPTER 12—

PENSACOLA TO SANFORD

The Navy rotates men…and their wives
and they go where needed, when needed
and ask no questions. They live to serve.

Life had been comfortable in California, so it was with some misgivings that Jan learned that I had been rotated back to Pensacola in the fall of '58. This time, however, I returned with experience and seniority, including a raise in pay. Also, Jan had fully adapted being a Navy wife and found that her pleasant smile and easy laughter brought friends wherever we went. We found a better house, a two story, large brick structure on the bayou, a proper venue for an ambitious young officer and his wife.

I was assigned to teach Pre-Flight Aerodynamics to cocky young Naval officers who reminded me of myself less than five years earlier. With some 450 carrier landings under my belt, I admit that I strutted with confidence, and was the object of whispered awe and great respect. I truly enjoyed my role as instructor.

Often I would take one of my students at a time aloft in a T-28 to demonstrate rolls, dives, and other spectacular maneuvers.

I could see the lights go on in their minds. "So THIS is what you've been teaching!"

I also quickly made sure that I qualified in a small Piper Aztec. There were two on base, one each assigned to the Chief of Naval Air Training and the Chief of Naval Air Basic Training. Since I was qualified, I often was tapped to fly the two Admirals around on Navy business flights.

My wife, Jan, in the meantime was growing increasingly mournful that she had not been able to conceive, and I watched an underlying sorrow begin to color her days blue, so much so that I proposed that we adopt. We had just begun to explore possibilities when Jan glowed with femininity—pregnant at last! And in 1960, our only child, Julie, was born in the Pensacola Naval Hospital. The three years of shore duty and the birth of our child had cemented our lives and I was one contented man, but it wasn't to last.

Three years and move on. Jan was used to it now. Like all other Navy officers I expected it.

But with the whole world to see, Pensacola to Sanford?
Oh, come on!

You don't argue with the Navy.

I leased a one-story home with a big back yard and Florida louvered windows, set apart under palm trees in a safe community with other nearby young Navy families with small children where Julie could play freely without constant supervision. Our big picture window framed a spectacular view: Each time a launching occurred at Cape Canaveral, there it was, bursting skyward right before us. It is still imprinted on my visual brain.

They were good years there with our infant daughter and close friends…

CHAPTER 13—

THE ROOSEVELT AND THE SEA GULLS

*Sea gulls always follow ships
but sometimes the "gulls" are human.*

We lived in Sanford, Florida for three years and then my Squadron was assigned to the USS Roosevelt, attached to the 6th Fleet in the Mediterranean with two deployments, each to be six to eight months.

After much discussion, my wife and I reached a difficult decision. We closed up the house, and took Julie, now three years old, back to Jan's parents in Mt. Horeb. Julie had visited Mt. Horeb often in her short life, and Jan knew, much as she would miss her baby, that it would be a summer of play time with the many children near her parents' home.

The plan was that Jan, along with two other Navy wives, Beatrice Garcia and Carolyn Dennison, would go to Europe and follow the ship from Spain to Turkey or wherever it put into port, and meet their husbands. They decided to call themselves the "Sea Gulls," the time-tested name for Navy wives who had followed ships to be with their husbands.

Jan was to have the experience of her lifetime. Well after the Roosevelt embarked for Europe, the three women flew to Luxembourg. From there Jan took the train to Zurich, Switzerland to a hotel where she was to meet me.

My telegram awaited her: "SKIPPER DEAD COME TO NICE SUISSE HOTEL CONFIRMED FOR 22ND JULY. MEET THERE. SCOTT." She was exhausted and in shock. She had never traveled abroad before, certainly not alone. She spent the night in the Zurich hotel, sunk in the security of the deep feather comforters and in the morning picked herself up and took the train to Nice.

By luck, and the fact that I had impressed my skipper, I was promoted to Executive Officer—which meant additional duties which increased my administrative work load and demanded more of my time than had been expected.

As the most junior ever executive officer of a fully deployed Heavy Attack Squadron in the Atlantic—Mediterranean Area for a six or more month cruise aboard an aircraft carrier in the U. S. 6th Fleet, my beautiful wife and I enjoyed a VAH-11 squadron party in Naples, Italy. Heavy Attack Eleven was known as "the Checkertails."

I still had to fly my scheduled flights.

At the time, I was told, and understood, that the need for airborne refueling pilots pushed aside the planned Heavy Attack Nuclear Weapons Delivery tasks which had been the original reason for the deployment.

Recently, I learned otherwise.

The A3B bombers deployed on carriers in the Atlantic Ocean were switched to tanking duty for an entirely different reason. In retrospect, it was a highly classified change performed without press releases and without informing anyone involved—except perhaps the skippers of the ships involved.

What happened was that all nuclear weapons on the carriers and other surface vessels were modified and transferred to the nuclear submarine fleet to be carried and delivered as—and if—required for defense of the United States. None of us knew when and where the weapons were removed. No one suspected anything. But by 1963 all weapons had been removed from surface ships and put aboard nuclear submarines.

There were important advantages in the secret repositioning of nuclear weaponry. The nuclear submarine fleet now could disperse the U. S. nuclear weapons arsenal in marine locations scattered around the earth. Potential enemies could no longer locate, inventory, or be certain of where the nuclear submarines and weapons were. Submarines could be relocated in short order without surfacing for months at a time.

Stealth and invisibility strengthened U. S. armed potential immeasurably to give us a necessary advantage if wartime with the Soviets would have occurred.

Since the end of WWII American aircraft carriers had become highly vulnerable to armed attack by any enemy possessing a highly skilled air force and a nuclear weapons capability. In the serious major war—the one that never came—I shudder to think how vulnerable our carriers would have been.

I was the most junior officer as a Lt. Commander who had ever successfully deployed for a whole cruise in an East Coast Heavy Attack Squadron, and I loved the position and the responsibility. It was a true learning experience. As a buffer between the Commanding Officer and the enlisted men, I learned the arts of building morale which was to stand me in good stead after my retirement when I studied for a doctorate in business administration and worked in industry.

In addition to these duties, I also had regular aircraft tanker assignments.

When a pilot from the Roosevelt would be on the return trip to the ship and there was an unexpected delay for any reason, it was my assignment to fuel the aircraft in midair.

I would orbit in my tanker in a left hand turn at 250 knots 20,000 feet above the ship, and when the pilot, now desperate and hoping to have enough fuel to land, would see the flashing green lights of the tanker, he would rendezvous on the port side of the tanker. I would then tell him to line up behind me. He would then maneuver through the wake of my aircraft and thrust the probe on the front of his aircraft into the aluminum feathered basket at the end of the hose extending from my bomb bay. When it locked in place, we would begin to fuel his bird. If the pilot had problems, I would talk him in.

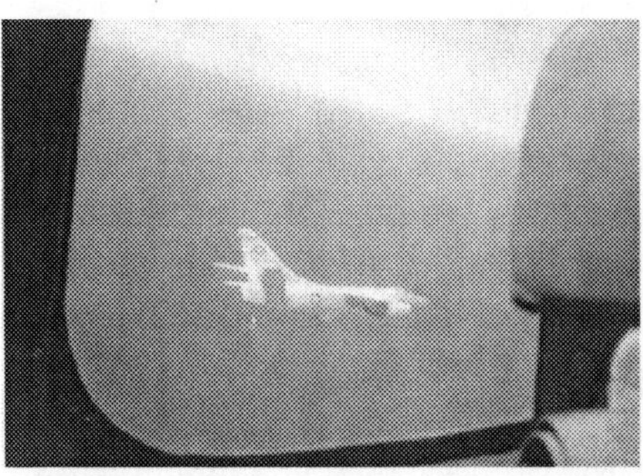

Tanking another aircraft in mid-flight required skill on the part of two pilots. As the receiving pilot in this set of pictures, I lined up my aircraft to be fueled behind the tanker and maneuvered my aircraft to insert my fueling probe into the tanker's refueling basket. It was exacting flying on the part of two pilots. No room for errors.

Almost there! Bulls eye! Perfect connection!

I became the most popular pilot in the sky, particularly at night. After a few nights of tanking, I never had to buy a drink at a bar.

During the two deployments on the Roosevelt, I was credited with more than 20 saves. This meant that the pilot had so little fuel left that he could not go to any airfield and was so low on fuel that the aircraft would go down without the tanking.

Sometimes the problem was language communication with the air fields, and sometimes the foreign tower or approach control men were obnoxious and didn't care whether the pilots landed or not. Other times, the weather was socked in and the runway lights were off.

When a pilot was too low on fuel to land on shore, I would be called in to fuel him in flight so the pilot could make it back to the carrier. Many a desperate pilot breathed easier at the sight of the steady turns of my tanker.

All Roosevelt pilots knew my tanker after my plane captain stenciled a "Caution" on the tail end of my fuselage. Every pilot that I refueled could not avoid reading the sign as he was about to plug into my refueling hose. "NOT TOO CLOSE. I HAVE GAS."

Some pilot laughed so hard they actually lost their refueling connection and had to plug in a second time. One laughed so hard when he finally registered what the sign said, that his probe fell out of the refueling basket AFTER he had started receiving fuel.

The usual pilot comment back in the Ready Room was, "That sign is an absolute gas!"

Jan again adapted, made new friends, learned to go to the USO to check the whereabouts and expected destinations of the Roosevelt, learned to read timetables in many languages, and like a sea gull, followed the ship. It was to Nice, then off to Naples by train. She and the other wives played bridge on the train, much to the amusement of French and Italian men, who hung over their shoulders to observe this oddity.

In Naples they checked into the Hotel Mediterranean in Center City a few blocks from the fleet landing and near the USO. The hotel owners were very considerate of the young Navy wives, charging them single rates any night the husbands were not in the rooms. The young women lived frugally, eating cheese and crackers for breakfast, washing out their clothes in the bidet, choosing the least expensive meals at small trattorias, saving all their money for the times when the men were ashore for evenings out in fancy restaurants.

One of the most romantic was a mountaintop inn overlooking Naples when we danced under the stars. Jan, a little more venturesome than the other two, and with financial assistance from her parents, went by train to explore Venice and Vienna.

When the Sea Gulls learned at the USO that the Roosevelt would dock in Athens, they packed their bags and took the train there. Again, they found people in the USO who were helpful and friendly who helped them find rooms in small pensions. Then it was back to Nice, then to Athens, to Istanbul, to Taranto, Italy, to Messina, Sicily. Where the ship went, our Sea Gulls followed.

A month after her two friends went home, Jan rented a car with two other women whose husbands were on the Roosevelt but not in the Squadron with me, and began following the ship by car instead of train.

In port, I often had duty every other day and could come ashore on alternate days off. Other evenings, Jan would take the Liberty Boat, along with many other families, out to the ship to have dinner with me there.

Sometimes the women would arrive at a pensione and wait…and wait…and wait. But while they waited, they also had a good time. One evening the three went to a five star hotel in Athens and were sitting at a bar, when a man approached with a proposition—an innocent adventure, it developed.

"Would you three ladies like to go to the Plaka and see a real Greek night?" They looked from one to the other, seeking approval, and then, collectively decided to chance it.

He escorted them from taverna to taverna for Greek dancing, resine, oozo, dolmas, and a whole range of authentic foods.

The ship was then due to dock at Naples, so, suitcases packed, they moved to Naples.

There was a United Nations Club on the outskirts of Naples where they could have dinner and dance with international officers from any ship in port—this time the Ben Jolie. There were three handsome young Naval officers at the next table—submariners, it developed—who asked to join the women. They danced the night away. By chance, a pilot who was a Carrier on Board (COD) delivery person to carriers, was seated at the next table. The next morning, we three husbands were free to come ashore. We knew all about the evening of dancing…before breakfast. Our wives were more than a little chagrined!

I had no way of contacting my wife and would not have been allowed to tell her if we could have talked, so she and her friends had to rely on scuttlebutt. The rumors came that the Roosevelt was on its way to Rhodes. So the Sea Gulls went to Rhodes. Then the rumors came that the Roosevelt was on its way to Athens. The three decided to take a very junky aircraft to Athens.

I became a Double Centurion on this ship. This photo of the USS Roosevelt (CVA 42), clearly shows the angled deck which was invented by the British Royal Navy and adopted for U.S. carriers in 1954. With this, the planes could take off and land without crashing into parked aircraft.

One of the girls was looking out the window. Look below!" she exclaimed. "It's the Roosevelt!" And there she was, headed for Rhodes!

What else was there to do? They spent their meager savings to take the same junky little aircraft back to Rhodes.

Our reward was an uninterrupted five days together in a small hotel overlooking the old walled city. We rented a car, drove into the interior to see the ruins of Rhodes. We passed a women carding wool and came to a country tavern where men were doing Greek dancing in the middle of a picture postcard day. Those were magic moments. It was an idyllic summer. Jan had no idea where I was flying to when she was not with me. It was as if we were dating again. Free of responsibility. A summer of fun.

It ended dramatically.

Jan was in Naples again, waiting for the ship, when she learned that it had thrown a propeller blade and would soon be on its way back to New Jersey.

I suddenly appeared with two weeks leave and a VW that a friend had asked to be delivered to Paris to be shipped to the U. S. It was a final honeymoon through the tapestry of Europe: Florence, Lake Como, the Alps, the Moselle Valley, the French champagne countryside where Jan's father had fought, Verdun, and three days in Paris.

Jan's parents drove to New Jersey with our lovely daughter Julie where Jan and I met them at the Roosevelt's dry dock. The four of them drove back to Mt. Horeb, through the flaming red-gold hills of fall, a touching finale to a summer to be treasured.

I remained aboard the USS Roosevelt in dry dock at Bayonne, New Jersey and resumed my duties as Squadron Executive Officer. The carrier had a new propeller blade installed and soon steamed back to the 6th Fleet in the Mediterranean Sea. All this carrier travel was performed at the time to avoid using the only dry dock in the Mediterranean Sea that was large enough to accept the 55,000 ton USS F. D. Roosevelt, CVA-42.

Since, at the time, President Charles de Gaulle was occupied with his "Americans Go Home" policy, the U. S. Navy decided it would not be prudent to let France have custody of our carrier in a French dry dock. Hence, the unscheduled round trip to dry dock in New Jersey.

All of us aboard agreed with the U.S. Department of Defense that the time and effort compensated for the French arrogance and lack of national appreciation for saving their posteriors in two calamitous world wars! The carrier with its air wing finished the scheduled cruise and returned to Mayport, Florida.

We were then reunited as a family in our home in Sanford, Florida

CHAPTER 14—

AN ASIDE ON HURRICANES

I was always amused at the reaction of residents in harm's way in Florida
and was always proud to count my wife as one of the calm, organized ones.

The weather was and is an integral part of living in Florida, and every summer and fall the predictable hurricanes came. There were always warnings in advance, but no one could prepare completely for the force of violent Nature unleashed and rampant.

As one of the most experienced pilots available, I was drafted into an experimental cloud seeding project that hoped to tame hurricanes while Jan was left to her own resources to prepare the house as best she could for the impending storm

The intensity of hurricanes over Florida during the late 50's and through the mid 60's was quite severe, though not as much so as the recent hurricanes of 2005. The storms spawned in the Caribbean Sea and usually progressed generally westward along the Lesser Antilles and northward clockwise past or over Cuba toward Florida. The storms were fueled and intensified over the Gulf of Mexico. Occasionally a storm might veer unpredictably northward and make first major landfall somewhere north of Florida on the Southeastern seaboard. Sometimes a hurricane would veer westward and churn into the Gulf of Mexico to threaten landfall in any Gulf state from Texas to Florida.

Storms were never predictable but always potentially life-threatening and severely destructive to vegetation and man-made objects.

The U. S. Weather Bureau was even then excellent at tracking the hurricanes. The Bureau kept citizens informed through news media, with frequent updates of storm intensity, possible path changes, winds, rainfall, lightning, sea wave intensities, tides, and possible flooding.

I was always amused at the reaction of residents in harm's way in Florida.

First, there were the "come what may" folks who would throw wild parties that lasted until the danger had passed. Such parties, however, it was interesting to note, were always at the home of the couple whose house sat on the highest elevation—for obvious reasons!Second, there were the "panic button" folks. They bought every piece of lumber, fiberboard and plywood that was available from any and all sources. All overstuffed furniture was carried to the highest locations within their homes. Pets, high value items, luggage, and dependents were poured into every operable vehicle that had a qualified driver. All house windows and many doors were boarded up and battened down.

The final action then began: A panic-stricken mass exodus of such proportions that caused severe congestion and jamming of all roads and highways in the storm's probable path. This meant at that time that emergency vehicles could not travel to places where they were most urgently needed.

Since then, planning and public education has improved traffic control and emergency procedures, although as we all know, the New Orleans hurricanes showed we are still badly remiss in our efforts.

Finally, there were the calmer, better organized planners. These prepared their homes and properties for probable high winds, intense rainstorms and possible invasive flood waters early on, when the warnings came out. A significant majority of these people remained in their homes after they had done all they could to minimize damage from the onslaught of 100 mile plus winds, intense rains, loss of electrical power, scarcity of potable water, lightning strikes, or flood damage. This choice was usually relatively safe but always nerve racking.

I was always proud to count my wife as one of these.

Wives of military pilots stationed at air bases subject to possible visits by hurricanes noted that fair and equal treatment of pilots and their dependents was not always the norm. When a hurricane approached or threatened an air field, pilots were ordered to fly all aircraft northward or inland out of harm's way—sans wives, children, and other dependents!

Doubtless, the anonymous senior Navy official who authored the slogan, "The Navy takes care of its own," did not wish to step forward and defend the statement when a hurricane was pending...

But Jan had learned to cope and even to find pleasure in the wild lashings of the rain against the snug security of our brick walls.

CHAPTER 15—

A RIDE TO REMEMBER: OCTOBER, 1963

So what was I doing during the hurricane season?
The plan was this: A Navy crew was to fly a Navy bomber
into a hurricane and at pre-designated positions
open the bomb bay and drop silver iodide and
other crystalline chemicals into the storm.
It sounded hazardous but controllable.

"You have five minutes for this briefing," I had said quietly when we met the briefing teams. "Weather's coming in."

I knew my growing tension was apparent, but I kept control. "Seeding a hurricane is hazardous business."

Although I had thoroughly studied what would be expected of us, I also knew this final briefing could be quite important.

I make it a point not to display anger when I fly because it is a distraction and a waste of energy, but there are rare times when a raised voice and a touch of profanity are not only important, but vital. This proved to be one of those times.

It was October 1, 1963. Our aircraft had been met at NAS Key West by a Navy carryall to take the three of us in the crew to the Operations Building where our final preflight briefing on weather was to take place.

Seven of us were now clustered in one of those oversized, under-furnished windowless rooms that served for any function as needed. All dozen or so of the chairs were dissimilar. On the two tables were strewn the dozens of Caribbean Area charts that showed the projected storm path and the hurricane area. The 15 foot ceilings in this cavernous warehouse-like building exuded no feeling of professionalism. A wooden, varnished desk in one corner begged for refinishing. A black, antiquated rotary telephone perched on the tired desk. I do not know if it was connected to the outside world; it never rang. All bulkheads (walls) were painted the Navy's standard, bilious, light green.

This was definitely not a showpiece that a host organization would be proud to display, and this had surprised me, considering the importance of the mission we had been asked to undertake.

The weather briefing man from the National Oceanographic Atmospheric Administration (NOAA) had come and gone, so his charts lay scattered at random across the cluttered table. What he had explained—clearly and completely—had left me tense and with a feeling of apprehensive urgency.

I pretended to study the charts, although I understood well the frightening nastiness they indicated. The storm was stronger than anyone would have anticipated and was on the move. The clock was running out.

Four representatives from the contractor had wandered in to join my crew and me. The uniformed Airfield Operations Duty Officer came in, introduced himself, briefly discussed a construction area on a taxi way that was to be avoided, shook hands all around and sat at one side, arms crossed, his face noncommittal, telling us clearly with his body language that he was present only to remain informed.

Three of the four reps were in their early forties, dressed in khakis or jeans and work shirts, since they had just come from checking out the special equipment on the aircraft. Their clothing was damp from the rain outside and from their sweat in the thick, sweltering humidity.

Before the briefing group could disburse, the foreman, who was not scheduled to do any briefing, rose to his feet and stated that he had a "few important comments" to make. The man had the air of someone in authority. He was a bit older than the other three, about 50, with a slight pot belly, graying temples, and a receding hairline. A battered briefcase was over-stuffed with dog-eared wet papers. His business suit under a Dick Tracy trench coat was wet and rumpled.

I pointedly looked at my watch.

His uninvited, unscheduled briefing began with a personal, proud, self-introduction. "I hope all of you are as excited and enthused by our hurricane seeding project as I am," he said. "I am informed we have an excellent flight crew and aircraft"

I moved restlessly, which he must have heard, but he did not look up or make any eye contact with anyone.

"My tech rep who is flying along in the cockpit with the air crew can field any questions the air crew may have about the payload in the bomb bay and electrical switching for crystalline disbursement from the canisters."

That was the first I had heard that anyone other than our crew would be in the aircraft. I held my tongue, and scowled at the tech rep the foreman had indicated.

The younger man smiled lopsidedly, apparently calm and unafraid. I wasn't happy with this unexpected development, but I could live with it.

Time was racing. The important thing was to get our bird into the air.

Then, without looking up, the foreman continued, "The chemical insertions are to be made at 10,000 feet"

It was then that I could contain myself no longer.

In my best controlled voice, seething with disgust and disbelief, I looked each representative in the eye and said, "You corporate cavaliers! You suffer a woeful lack of knowledge and an insipid misunderstanding of flying in severe weather. If my Navy superiors had not ordered me to give you all reasonable support, I would send you twits out of here running!"

I slammed my fist down on the wooden table, sending charts and weather sheets flying. I lowered my voice.

"Now, I'll tell you what is really going to happen!"

I was so angry that my voice lowered two octaves.

"The aircraft commander always makes all decisions affecting flight. Here is my first decision even before we launch." I was completely cold. "You'd better damn well believe this! All insertions will be made at a minimum altitude of 15,000 feet. In a storm like this one, vertical down drafts can slam our 36 ton bomber like a toy. We'll experience high "g" forces and altitude changes of more than 6,000 feet per minute!! With no visibility outside the cockpit and turbulent air, we could crash into the sea. We could be forced below 5000 feet. Our engines could ingest lumber, sheet metal, palm trees, flying vegetation…anything! Survival probabilities at such a low altitude on a day like this are very poor! This briefing is finished! All crew, man your aircraft!"

I stalked out.

The Operations Duty Officer could not contain himself any longer. He left the briefing room chuckling and grinning from ear to ear.

My enlisted flight engineer said in a loud, clear voice as we exited, "God, Commander, that was beautiful!"

The contractor foreman left the room. I never saw him again

We would drop the crystals at 15,000 feet.

Months before, the "weather guesser" types, as we pilots referred to them, had conjured up a plan to experiment with chemically seeding hurricanes from an aircraft in an attempt to diminish the amounts of moisture carried aloft by the giant storms. The scientists at NOAA hoped to learn how and where it might be possible to influence rain bursts during a hurricane to drop their huge quantities of water over the open ocean, away from inhabited land masses and perhaps minimize the horrendous damage inflicted by these terrible storms.

Hurricanes are killers. Winds over 100 miles per hour scream menacingly, tugging trees out by their rain soaked roots, peeling roofs off buildings, splintering windows, and tossing cars around, and then mixing the fractured debris in a maelstrom of disaster. Rain bursts thunder like powerful waterfalls and drive needles of water penetrating deep into the earth until hills become thick, smothering brown liquid forces that roll an avalanche of unstoppable, smothering mud down over homes, fields, trees, vehicles, animals, and helpless men, women, and children. Waves 30 feet high crash over beaches to suck away buildings and streets and everything in their path. Above, the cacophony of thunder and the crash of lightning resonate like some demonic orchestra playing a symphony of human destruction.

If the incredible tide of rain that is part of a hurricane could be diverted out over the ocean, the reasoning went, this could diminish flooding, mud slides, crop destruction, and minimize the subsequent death and disease—a noble, but seemingly unrealistic undertaking.

NOAA had hired a contractor to examine and research this theory for practicality, controllability, and effectiveness. The contractor, following the best models available in that time,—before our present-day computer ubiquitousness,—had designed an experiment—a plan for careful cloud seeding of the next hurricane.

They had waited for their hurricane—ever more impatiently—for three months, spending the time outfitting a Navy aircraft with the canisters of silver iodide.

Ordinarily, there are several hurricanes during a season, but this year, by chance, none had developed late enough to be available after completion of the extensive modifications, configuration, and installation of special equipment in the hurricane seeding aircraft. The season soon would be over. The experiment was ready. Finally, all that was needed was the hurricane. And now that hurricane was coming.

The plan was this: A Navy crew was to fly a Navy bomber into a hurricane and at pre-designated positions open the bomb bay and drop carefully calculated amounts of silver iodide and other crystalline chemicals out of many canisters which would be attached to the bomb bay racks and associated hardware within the aircraft bomb bay.

NOAA needed the services of a highly experienced, multi-thousand flight hour crew and a very strong aircraft with a large bomb bay for disbursement of crystalline chemicals from canisters.

My crew and I fit the bill for the needed personnel.

The A3B was right for the aircraft. It could withstand high "g" forces, and its two Pratt and Whitney J-57-P-10 turbojet engines produced 10,000 lbs. of thrust each and had flown many times in heavy turbulence and torrential rains without flaming out. The aircraft could carry sufficient fuel to make the desired number of crystalline insertions within required time and distance constraints desired by the NOAA plan.

So our A3B had been selected and outfitted.

This day had been chosen by NOAA and agreed to in advance by the U. S. Navy. Our A-3B bomber and crew were never a designated entity in the NOAA inventory—only on a limited loan from the U. S. Navy.

We had launched our first leg of the journey before dawn on Oct. 1 from our base at NAS Sanford, Florida. We made an instrument descent and Ground Controlled Approach at NAS Key West in light rain and tricky, variable crosswinds during final approach and touchdown on the runway.

Another group of NOAA contractors were waiting to make last minute adjustments and checks on the bomb bay contents prior to our voyage into the hurricane maelstrom.

The storm center was predicted to be near Puerto Rico when we would make our initial, violent encounter with this angry storm and winds that already had intensified above and beyond any dimensions on the Beaufort Scale of wind force measurements.

We were the crew assigned the task and briefed on its difficulties. We were their hope and their guinea pigs. My navigator, my flight engineer and I were that crew. I had flown often with both men, and trusted them—as they did me.

We were a well coordinated team. We could read each other's thoughts and had developed our own language of hand signals to minimize use of cockpit transmissions that might block out vital radio communications while we were inside the "killer 'cane,"

NOAA's contractor crew of a half dozen technical representatives had worked feverishly that last fortnight of September installing chemical canisters in the bomb bay of the Navy aircraft at NAS Sanford, Florida. The canisters were designed to be actuated electrically and opened at the bottom permitting the chemical crystalline contents to be dropped and disbursed into the atmosphere. Each of the dozens of canisters was approximately four feet high and about 14 inches in diameter. They were attached to a specially engineered support rack, which, in turn, was anchored to integral bomb rack hardware. A maze of electrical wires was "jury rigged" and ran every which way up to the cockpit.

When I first saw it, I instructed the contractor installation foreman that he had to tie his hodgepodge of wires into secure bundles that could be anchored to the bomb bay interior or all wires would be either ripped off or shorted out the first time the bomb bay doors were opened in a 500 mph relatively quiet wind.

"Gosh," he had said, "I don't think we considered that." At that moment, I knew that the job had to be carefully monitored and approved by my squadron ordnance officer and maintenance officer.

The first indication that this might be the awaited hurricane came when Weather reported that a tropical atmospheric disturbance had formed between the equator and 10 degrees North latitude, drawing energy from the heat of the 80 degree Fahrenheit or higher ocean waters. It had begun its typical northern-hemisphere counter clockwise spin that signaled the development of the waited storm. Everything was falling in place. Hurricane Flora had yet to be named, but had heralded her arrival.

As always, thinking ahead and anticipating outcomes, I had requested that air operations at Key West contact NAS Roosevelt Roads on the eastern extreme of Puerto Rico to assure that no storm damage had occurred that would preclude an emergency or unscheduled landing (with instrument approach and GCA landing) by an A3B type of aircraft. Also, I had requested that their runway arresting gear be checked and ready in case an aircraft with hurricane damage landed at an unscheduled arrival time.

NAS Roosevelt Roads had an 11,000 foot runway and excellent maintenance ground support. I felt it was my best choice for a landing east of the hurricane center that was moving westward. I had been assured I would receive confirmation in the cockpit before my takeoff, and I did.

There were numerous other airfields with sufficient length runways, instrument approaches and some with minimal available maintenance support. Unfortunately, all of them were in the probable path of Flora.

The storm remained unrelenting.

The time was rapidly approaching to take off and meet Flora head on. The aircraft configuration was fine-tuned and ready; my air crew was thoroughly briefed and prepared to accept the challenge.

We were completely aware of the dangers. We all knew that if we had to jump out of that aircraft into Flora that would be our final chapter—survival chances would be slim, improbable and none!

Once we were in the cockpit the possibilities were not mentioned, but they were in everyone's thoughts.

Flora put us on notice that she was out there lurking, waiting for our arrival. The grayness succumbed to moderate, steady rain. It was all business now. Nothing was said except that which was necessary to complete preflight check lists and communicate with ground control. I requested taxi clearance and was cleared to the duty runway to hold. Before I reached the end of the runway, ground control switched me to tower frequency. The tower cleared us onto the runway and for immediate takeoff.

Less that one minute later in heavy rain we were airborne, wheels up, flaps coming up, turning to our assigned collision course with Flora and climbing. Our post flight check list was quickly completed.

I had instructed the flight engineer to strap the inexperienced tech rep into the flight engineer's regular seat, so he sat back to back with me. The flight engineer sat in the fourth position, atop the lower escape hatch, strapped to the rear cockpit bulkhead so he could keep an eye on the tech rep. The navigator was in his usual right seat position.

The air crew and tech rep observer relaxed as I remained quite preoccupied with headings, altitude, air speed, little to no visibility in light to moderately turbulent air. Our bird was performing in excellent fashion. We cruised north of Cuba in an easterly direction to stay out of Cuban airspace where Castro had refused us clearance. That paranoid dictator had everything to gain for the good of his country and people if our research could alleviate future hurricane destructive and killing forces that were about to destroy Cuban tobacco and sugar crops, cause more than 1300 Cuban fatalities and leave 175,000 Cuban citizens destitute in just this one hurricane! Yet he still refused clearance.

Behind me, I could hear, even over the jet engine noise, the tech rep miserably retching into the airsick bags we had provided.

Before we had taken off, I had told my crew to wear their oxygen masks and had quietly told my flight engineer to see that the tech rep did not wear his mask but had it attached on one side of his hard hat. My reasoning was that I was fully aware how air sick the tech rep might become, and I did not want him drowning in his own vomitous.

From the sounds behind me, I knew my decision was correct.

We turned southeast to pass along the northern coast of Hispaniola. This change of direction took us onto a course that more directly penetrated the hurricane and increased the turbulence we experienced. We now were on a collision course that was moving us more directly toward the eye of Flora.

The navigator was extremely busy measuring the very large wind drift numbers which tried to force us far off course to the north of our desired track as we penetrated the northwest quadrant of the hurricane. Turbulence continued to increase, and we flew in and out of numerous rain bursts along our flight path at 15,000 feet.

My eyes kept darting over the engine instruments checking for any indications of possible compressor stall or flame out from the thousands of pounds of rainwater per hour that my twin turbojet engines were obviously ingesting. We were penetrating the colossal storm at a ground speed of approximately 5 ? nautical miles per minute. Those wonderful jet engines were consuming JP-5 jet fuel and rainwater and kept right on producing the life saving thrust needed to keep us airborne.

My navigator got a good radar fix from the coastline of the Dominican Republic and the eye of Flora. Following a course correction, we soon reached "Drop Point One."

The navigator opened the bomb bay doors 10 seconds before the scheduled release. When the doors opened, Flora roared lustily into the bomb bay. I felt the aircraft decelerate and shudder and I instinctively added thrust to maintain constant air speed.

The navigator punched the number one release button and the Venturi effect sucked the crystalline chemicals out of canisters and bomb bay into the .65 Mach air stream. Seconds later, the navigator closed the bomb bay doors after completing our first seeding insertion.

I turned to a course that would take us to "Drop Point Two" and adjusted air speed and altitude for the second insertion. By now the tech rep had filled two of his airsick bags and was working on his third. The navigator alerted the crew that we would penetrate the hurricane eye en route to our next drop point.

What an eerie sensation it was to tumble out of the turbulence through the solid, opaque wall of the storm into Flora's eye! I estimated the calm center to be at least five to seven miles in diameter, maybe more.

It was dead calm in there—no wind, no rain, no turbulence, not a breath of air. Below, the Caribbean seemed still—sparkling and calm. Above, the open sky was streaked with clouds and lighted by an intermittent sun. We had been briefed, but the absolute calm, the utter peace, the supernatural quiet was still unexpected.

"Spectacular," the navigator murmured in hushed tones.

Our tech rep leaned his head against the cockpit window. His face was bleached the color of a cadaver's, and there were blue circles under his eyes.

"Please, God," I heard him half whisper. "Don't go back in there again."

I called my flight engineer and asked him to replenish the tech rep's supply of airsick bags. That was all we could do to help him.

In spite of the tech rep's plea, we bored into the high winds, rain bursts, and turbulence on the other side of the eye as we prepared for our second chemical insertion.

I anticipated some difficulty on this leg of the flight as we cruised upwind directly into a headwind of 150 mph with gusts to 170 mph, rain bursts, and vertical drafts of wind that created high 'g' forces on crew and aircraft. I concentrated on using smooth and moderate control movements to keep correcting aircraft attitude, altitude, heading, and air speed. I was not going to over-stress the control surfaces and the main strength members of our aircraft if that could be avoided.

I was so busy concentrating on smooth control, that I was startled by the sudden, intensified vertical up and down drafts of air.

Flora was playing with us. We were her mouse.

The aircraft seemed to go straight up, beyond human control, as if a hand had plucked us out of the horizontal and thrown us skyward like a ball.

My hard hat jammed down over my eyes and my oxygen mask was pushed down, almost off my face. My hands were torn from the controls and pressed downward. My whole body was compressed. I felt that my neck was being flattened into my spine.

I frantically shoved the mask upward against the hard hat so I could see the aircraft's attitude. My head banged against the cockpit, but I had the controls in my hands again.

Then just as quickly, we were thrown nose down and rolled 170 degrees—almost inverted. Flora had tossed us downward.

The rate of climb/descent instrument pegged a 6,000 feet a minute descent. We had been at the peak of a deadly roller coaster. Now we dropped heartrendingly fast.

The crew let out involuntary shouts.

The strap of my hard hat bit fiercely into my throat.

My eyes blurred as the blood rushed from my feet to my head.

The navigator struggled to see the radar screen. My flight engineer was either swearing or praying aloud. The tech rep let out an anguished moan.

I would not over-stress our bird with too much control. We passed 10,000 feet altitude in the plunging, stomach wrenching dive. I rapidly rolled the aircraft right side up and quickly started a 5 'g' pull-up schedule; so every man in our bird suddenly was five times his normal weight. I prayed that this maneuver would be sufficient to keep us above all the foreign objects that were sailing around closer to the ocean surface. I then added another 'g' to our pullout schedule to stay above 5,000 feet altitude.

I looked at my rate of descent. It neared zero. The altimeter read 4,600 feet. For the first time I felt confident we would make it.

The bird responded. We started to climb. For an instant I flashed back to my earlier, stubborn, almost intransigent, resolve and knew that the extra 5,000 feet had saved us from crashing into the ocean.

We then encountered an updraft at just the right moment, and we rode it up several thousand feet out of the foreign object damage probability zone. I again adjusted course, altitude and air speed shortly before our next insertion point, and we dropped our payload on schedule.

After that terrifying episode, the remainder of the flight was not as nightmarish, and I continued to make constant relatively moderate corrections well within the 'g' and stress limits of our main strength members and control surfaces. My patience paid dividends as we followed our flight plan to successful completion for the remaining insertions.

As we took up our first heading for home base, I saw the navigator visibly relax and heard the even breathing of my flight engineer—both obviously relaxed and relieved to have this mission almost over. I started an immediate climb to hopefully reduce engine ingestion of rain and avoid the violent vertical up and down drafts of turbulent air. The maneuver was reasonably successful.

We circumnavigated Cuban air space again on our passage homeward. My navigator complied with my request to come up on NAS Key West Approach control frequency and request a radar monitored descent with a "handoff" to Key West GCA for final approach and landing. It was professionally handled and completed as expected.

Flora kissed us goodbye from fluttering fingertips, with intermittent moderate to heavy rain bursts during our final approach and GCA.

The only comment heard by the crew as we touched down on the rain drenched runway was exclaimed by our very nauseous technical representative.

"Thank God!"

We burst into gales of nearly uncontrollable laughter, comic relief after a harrowing experience. That poor man had been coerced by his lack of knowledge of turbulent air flying, corporate chicanery and his own naiveté to "take his ride into hell and back" as he referred to it. He had contributed nothing, observed nothing, but thanks to the experienced crew, a fabulous aircraft, he had survived. Skill and luck again.

He showed a lot of class in the last analysis. He arose early on October 2 and saw us off on our return flight to NAS Sanford, Florida. He shook hands with all of us.

"I was too damned sick and scared to appreciate it during the flight, but I now realize that a highly qualified, professional crew brought me home safely," he said quietly. "Thank you all."

Later, I inquired about the results of the test. I was met with stony silence. I doubt that the results were significant. In my own analysis, dropping the contents of all those canisters in a hurricane of Flora's force and size was like a mouse peeing in the ocean and expecting to measure a rise in the tide.

I much later learned that, since the results did not fit the expected statistics because the hurricane was so much more violent than had been expected, that Project STORMFURY simply omitted any reference to the flight. They cited instead the seedings of Hurricane Edith in 1962, Beulah in 1963, and Debbie in 1969. The Navy moved on and Project STORMFURY died a natural and well deserved death in 1983. All of us in that aircraft were simply pawns to be used to try to prove their theories.

About the only thing that I personally learned was from our unlucky tech rep; what I learned was that when you think you are through vomiting, you can still vomit more.

But I don't think that is measurable or significant in the larger scheme of life.

CHAPTER 16—

LIFE IN ATSUGI: 1964–1969

To know a country, you must live IN and OF it—
not on an American base, but in the land.

It was 1964 and I had been transferred to Atsugi, Japan…the far side of the world in geography and in culture.

We moved into temporary quarters in a small Japanese hostelry close to the Main Gate of the U. S. Naval Air Station, Atsugi, Japan. Our first night there was a real shock. We were settled in our room getting our three year old Julie ready for bed when huge thumping noises actually shook the walls! No one had informed us that there was a karate and tae kwan do classroom right overhead!

The next morning I put on a very stern face and assumed my command voice to inform the hotel manager that my family would move out immediately and would notify the Navy of the extremely unsatisfactory situation. Further, I would assure that his hotel would be removed from the list of hotels that qualified for Navy transient families. The harried manager quickly agreed that there would be no classes after 6 p.m.—and kept his promise.

Sometimes a command presence is a wonderful talent when properly executed!

Less than one week later, I moved my wife and daughter into an American style cottage that had been constructed by an American man betrothed to a Japanese national. This arrangement eliminated red tape and administrative delays.

It was a one-story cottage with two bedrooms, a bathroom with American plumbing, a small kitchen, and a smaller maid's room where we installed our American washer and clothes dryer. We were so comfortable there that we remained in our Japanese-American cottage for our entire five year tour.

The Naval Air Facility at Atsugi is composed of 1,249 acres and lies in the center of the Kanto Plain of Honshu, the main island of Japan. It is surrounded by farmland and forest, pine trees and underbrush.

It was built in 1938 in anticipation of American bombing raids of the Japanese mainland and was used to train the Emperor's pilots. As a result, there were many underground defense facilities with a series of tunnels. In 1950, the Navy selected Atsugi as its major Naval Air Station in the Far East and restored and developed what had been buildings and facilities in very poor condition. They had added a theater, a bowling alley, and a swimming pool, so that by the time I was assigned there, it was a fully functioning base.

While Jan was adapting to this foreign culture, I was being integrated into VQ-1, the spying arm for the Navy. In less than two weeks, I was fully occupied and fell into the squadron routine—much of which was classified because of the electronic reconnaissance missions in which we were involved.

The squadron reconnoitered Russia, North Korea, and China in the Sea of Japan. In addition we were part of the reconnaissance of the China mainland, Hainan Island, and all of North Vietnam in South East Asia. We were often assigned other special reconnaissance missions for intelligence agencies of the Federal government.

When my family and I first arrived in Japan, South East Vietnam was in utter chaos. The U. S. Air Force ruled the roost and jealously went to great lengths to attempt to prevent any other U. S. Military forces from participating even though their help was vital in conducting the war there. It was so obvious that soon thereafter, some very heavy political and Navy clout opened up South Vietnam to the Navy.

As an example, in 1964, VQ-1 was tasked to reconnoiter North Vietnam with as many as 100 electronic sorties per year. But to make life difficult for other Services, the U. S. Air Force claimed they had no available hangars, maintenance areas, buildings, barracks, revetments, etc.

The Navy was initially forced to deploy their aircraft and personnel to NAS Cubi Point, Luzon, Philippines. This forced the Navy aircraft to spend three and a half hours—round trip—on every mission before any intelligence gathering took place. This caused gross expenses for excess aviation fuel, aircraft maintenance, and unnecessary air crew fatigue.

Finally, some of the higher military commands came to their senses and worked out compromises so that conditions improved.

The VQ-1 Electronic Reconnaissance aircrews usually had a tour of eight to ten weeks in country and were stationed at DaNang Airbase in

South Vietnam. Then that crew returned to NAS Atsugi and regularly flew reconnaissance flights in the Sea of Japan targeting Russia, North Korea-even China. This was not what one might call R & R or crew rest, but nevertheless—that's the way it was.

For five years we lived in Atsugi, and I flew missions out of DaNang. During that time, along with two other officers, I rotated as the senior command officer as well as performing my duties as a pilot spy in the sky. It sounds glamorous today, but at the time, it was drudgery combined with sheer terror and extreme discomfort. General Sherman said that "War is Hell," and he could easily have been describing my professional life out of DaNang.

The way it worked was that I could either be assigned to fly my missions as a regular VQ-1 spy pilot, which meant a period in the sky of three or four hours, two or more times a day, Or, as Officer-in Charge, I could perform my administrative duties AND fly the same number of missions.

When it was my turn to shoulder the additional responsibilities, I would be given the "office" which was nothing more than a plywood partition in the BOQ (Bachelor Officers' Quarters.) From there I would file the administrative, maintenance, and discipline reports on the approximately 80 officers and 200 men under my command. There were daily, weekly, and monthly reports to be filed.

The Viet Cong and North Vietnamese Army made sure that we stayed alert by filling our nights with the raucous sound of the alarms that pulled us out of deep sleep to drag ourselves to the safety—and discomfort—of the bunkers. Often, when we went out on spy night flights, it was a struggle to keep alert. I was often sleepy and tired—but the flights were essential and the paper work had to be done.

The daily operational report logged in the numbers and types of missions flown and the code numbers for the pilots on each sortie. Everything was letters and numbers so it would have been unintelligible gobble-de-gook to an enemy that intercepted it.

Anyway, since we had a change of crews every week from Atsugi to DaNang, almost everything went by aircraft rather than by electronic communication. Sometimes, since communication was so jammed in South East Asia, if we had an important communication that had to go by wire, we would upgrade it from "confidential" to "secret." Otherwise, it might have taken a week or longer to get through.

When we lost an aircraft or crew, all communication would go through VQ-1.

One of the interesting—and troubling—aspects of the command position was the necessity of conducting courts martial, usually for drug related problems among enlisted men. Marijuana was everywhere and easily obtained. The men were young and far from the support systems of home and family. I had the Military Justice Manual as a guide, but often a case required and allowed a certain amount of discretion and common sense. But these men were on duty—25 hours a day, and drug usage was more than forbidden—it endangered others. As senior officer, I needed to be judge, jury, and counselor, holding a summary or special courts martial. If I could not resolve the problem at this level, or if the conduct was particularly egregious, I would refer it on to a special or general courts martial in Atsugi.

These and other discipline cases had to be written up and sent up the chain of command—whenever I could make the time between missions.

I didn't get a lot of sleep.

After I'd flown with VQ-1 for three years, I was tapped for Seabrine, at that moment, the most secret of the spying missions. Seabrine's task was to monitor all Russian deep space vehicles returning into the Earth's atmosphere for ocean recovery. We were tasked to record everything possible, electronically, during high altitude near-intercepts with the reentry vehicle flight path to touchdown—challenging and exciting!

By chance, the time I was summoned to Washington, D. C. for orientation for Seabrine, I was nursing a sick aircraft home from Atsugi along the Alaskan island chain toward San Francisco. It was one of those times when I was glad I didn't know how sick that bird was. I was assigned to deliver the aircraft to Overhaul and Repair (O & R) in my old stamping grounds at NAS Alameda.

We were about two hours out of Atsugi on what was expected to be an eight hour routine flight, when, without warning, the laminated glass and plexi-glass windscreen started peeling apart. Being cautious by nature, I always wore my visor.

My navigator did not. As the windshield disintegrated, pieces of it sliced into his eyes. Had that happened to me, we would not have been able to limp back to Atsugi and land.

My presence was needed in Washington, so for the first and only time in my 27 years of service, I flew commercially, first class, from San Francisco to Washington D.C.

I already had the highest security clearance which meant that the investigators had gone back to my childhood—back to Mt. Horeb—and acquaintances there.

"What did you do wrong?" they later asked me. "These FBI types

came into town and interviewed everybody. They wanted to know everything about you!"

Had I not had that top level clearance, I would never have been able
to monitor the progress of the Pueblo years later in the underground, top-
security room.

In Washington I passed through five levels of security including the
reading of my palm print and the scan of my pupils, before I was briefed as
the role of Seabrine and became acquainted with the people I'd be working
with.

When I walked into the briefing room, there on the wall was an eight
foot by 10 foot picture of Sputnik, which had shocked the U. S. armed services and the entire country by landing on the moon. The National Security
Agency had the capacity of intercepting the Russian telemetry and getting
the picture. Before the Russians did!

I was impressed.

I continued to be impressed. I would be sent to a spot in the sky—anywhere in the world—and lo, there was a Russian reentry vehicle.

How could they know? It finally dawned on me. The Seabrine radar
support system would keep track of the Russian reentry support ships, and
this gave them a specific locale on any ocean where they should deploy the
Seabrine aircraft in close proximity so we were available to be airborne
quickly when other indicators demonstrated the probability of a nearby
reentry.

In one instance, just at dawn in poor visibility, we were shadowing a
Soviet reentry vehicle and our ground radar experts had given us such
uncanny radar vectors and altitude assignment to position our aircraft in the
reentry vehicle path that we almost collided with the space craft.

My aircraft was in such close proximity that for an instant, all aboard
thought that we had been struck by lightning.

The spaceship roared by with horrendous supersonic shock waves that
abruptly shook our craft and painfully deadened our ears. The shock waves
were so intense that entire aircraft lurched and shuddered. For a split second the night was bright white. The concussion was so strong and unexpected that it deafened all hands aboard.

None of us knew what had happened!

I immediately did a complete scan of the instrument panel. The bird
was fine.

After our heart rates approached normal we reconstructed what had
happened. We orbited the recovery scene to record everything electronically and occasionally photographically.

Most of us had dull earaches and headaches for a few hours after that rendezvous from outer space! It was an amazing happening that was unlikely to ever again occur, but it certainly was testimony to the accuracy of our computer and radar experts in their quest for precision and outstanding professional performance.

Although I was never to see the printouts or readouts of the aircraft I flew, I knew how immensely important this gathering of secret information was to my country, and I was proud to be a part of it.

After that, most of the time I was VQ-1, spying on Russia, China, Vietnam, and the other hostile or potentially hostile countries in that part of the world.

Then I would be pulled away to become Seabrine. These were episodic assignments, dotting the VQ-1 background that was my primary duty out of Atsugi

Jan knew only that I would go out as VQ-1 or as Seabrine without knowing what I did or where I went. My job was secret and my instructions were to keep everything secret. And I did.

She was an intelligent, understanding Navy wife who adapted beautifully no matter what the demands.

Vice Admiral Highland presented me with one of my 20 air medals for flying as a spy in the sky in VQ-1. U.S. Navy Reconnaissance aircraft did not carry any kind of ordnance or gunnery which made the task exceptionally hazardous.

                    R. Scott Beat

We were not the first to be transferred to a very foreign land, of course, and the Navy was, and is, organized and helpful in a move of this dimension. We were given sponsors, a Navy officer and his wife—the Lenhardi's—from the Squadron who'd been there, done that, and who forced us to think in terms of "What do you need to bring with you? What can you find there?" We had opted to bring most of our furniture, to take our home with us. They were wonderfully helpful.

We had always resisted living in base housing, and our sojourn in this very foreign environment was made fascinating by the need to live away from the conformity of other Navy families.

The American style wonderful cottage which we leased was one of ten which had been built by an American betrothed to a Japanese woman. What that meant was an indoor, modern bathroom rather than a porcelain squat hole. It was wood beam and plaster construction outside with hardwood floors, two bedrooms and a maid's room (where we put our washer and dryer), far from the base, away from the city, out in the country. There, of course, the country was full of small houses on twisting streets.

The house reminded us of a cabin in northern Wisconsin, except that a Benjo ditch for waste water, and in some cases, sewage, ran in front of the house. No phone. No TV. Only Japanese neighbors. No way to get in touch with the base and that slice of America abroad without getting into the car and driving there.

There were other Navy families in the same prefecture, women and their children who were to become Jan's mainstay and support in the long stretches when I would be away—where I was and what I was doing, she was not allowed to know.

Jan, always conscientious, threw herself into adapting to the strange land. She learned enough Japanese from her English speaking maid, Masako San, to get by in the market and communicate with workmen for the help she needed.

The goldfish man came by and Julie and the neighboring Japanese children ran in response to his bell to buy yet one more black, gold, and white fish for the aquarium. A sweet potato man, with hot, steaming fragrant yams or the fish man with fresh fish on ice on his cart would bring out the housewives to bargain and buy. Each delivery man had his distinctive Japanese song or bell. The garbage man played classical music and the honey wagon, which collected the buckets from under the houses, announced his presence by the odor rather than the sound.

The Japanese thought then of the human body quite differently than the somewhat Puritanical American approach.

Jan had to adapt.

We discovered that one corner of the house had developed mildew that was destroying the wooden foundation, so the owner sent a crew of five men to make repairs. Jan was expecting them, but not quite as they came. The five workers climbed the steps to the porch and she answered the door. They bowed and smiled…and proceeded to take off all their clothing, all the way down to the briefest of g-strings. They neatly folded their clothing so it would not get dirty.

Jan took Julie into their bedroom and moved furniture in front of the door.

I thought the tale funny, but my wife didn't appreciate the humor.

There was a public bath down the street. Every evening men and women would go there to bathe and then walk home…nude, with only a towel, loosely wrapped, exposing parts that we never see on television even today.

Another time, the kitchen sink had stopped up and Jan walked a half block to the home of our handyman, a tiny, wizened man, sturdy and always helpful.

"Otska San," Jan called out.

He was in his steaming ofuro (very hot bath) behind his house in his yard.

He climbed out, bowed. "Oh, yes, Mama San, Otska come. Otska fix." Then he picked up his towel and dried his nude body thoroughly.

Jan soon learned that Japanese men were not at all interested in "foreign" women. She and I felt completely safe when she had to walk on the dark country roads, from the train at night.

The wives there were a cohesive group who took advantage of their opportunities and the misfortune of our required long absences. There were six Navy wives who lived nearby in Chuo Rinkin: Ethel Vanice, Fran Powell, Susie Roberts, Tamiko Christman, Nancy Wood and Jan. Together they flew to Hong Kong, to Bangkok, to Kuala Lampur, Singapore, and Taiwan.

Once when she had been in Bangkok for three days, we later learned that I too had been there overnight.

With three or four travelers, the women found it economical to rent a guide from the hotel in each town.

The Officers' Wives Club took one day tours on the speedy trains and saw such things as a Geisha Training School where young girls learned the arts of pleasing men.

One of the most triumphant days of Jan's life there was when she mastered the complicated and formerly incomprehensible Freeway system in Tokyo on one of her shopping excursions.

When I was home between deployments, we went skiing together in the northernmost part of Japan on Hokaido Island and the Japanese Alps on the island of Honshu…There were long stretches, however, when I was away.

They would come to get me sometimes in the middle of the night. I might be back by morning, or sometimes I would be gone for two weeks. Jan knew not to inquire too deeply.

It was the same for all the wives. They knew their husbands were flying spy aircraft, because there were sometimes fatal accidents, and the grim news flowed darkly through their tight community.

Jan rarely complained, but the loneliness preyed on her, and I sympathized without being able to help.

"I got so tired of potluck dinners with wives and children," Jan today recalls. "We felt so isolated sometimes. Potlucks and bridge. Bridge and potlucks."

During these five years, when I was a spy in the sky in VQ-1, and intermittently a pilot in the Seabrine task group I was always on the edge of disaster

I flew a recon aircraft that photographed and recorded each action the Russians and Chinese made, as well as other belligerent, maverick governments which were possible treats to world peace.

Jan knew nothing of my comings and goings—where I flew or what I did.

I was all over the world of the East, flying hazardous assignments, in an aircraft that photographed and recorded each action the Russian or Chinese Communists made.

Julie prospered and grew, from a three year old to an eight year old in the five years we were there. Jan's background as a kindergarten teacher helped with the transitions. Julie attended an American preschool and later the US Government primary school. All the teachers were young, enthusiastic women with at least three years of experience who had signed on for the adventure, or perhaps to look for an officer husband. When Julie returned to a Stateside school, she was up to or ahead of her classmates.

Julie played with neighborhood children and became fluent in Japanese.

"There was no keeping her clean," Jan recalls. "It was black volcanic soil, and once a child sat in it, the pants and underpants never were white again." Shoes came off at the door—for adults and children—to avoid tracking in.

We lived two lives, my wife and I, and it was good that she was never fully aware of the close calls I had with death.

CHAPTER 17—

SOME SKILL; SOME LUCK-
July, 1964

The following day the seemingly endless war continued.
My aircrew and I flew back into the Gulf of Tonkin.

The torrid Philippine sun and tropical high humidity were unrelenting in July 1964. The short walk to my jet reconnaissance aircraft opened every pore on my head and body and sapped my energy. I labored through a preflight inspection of the "bird" as my six man air crew joined me in the hot shade under the wing of our aircraft.

We discussed last minute details of our forthcoming mission while our aircraft maintenance crew topped off aircraft liquid oxygen supply and buttoned up any inspection access panels that remained open."

"Can't wait to get up there," Jack Poss, my usually uncomplaining captain, groused.

I ignored him, though I also agreed with him. I always enjoyed flying with Jack. He had such a positive attitude, and he thought ahead and anticipated what needed to be done—an approach that makes a pilot's job significantly safer and easier.

Every physical movement was a chore in the blazing afternoon sun radiating off the aircraft parking ramp. The concrete became blistering hot within a few hours after dawn and remained that way into each evening. My flight suit, which I had donned only two hours before, was already soaked and salt encrusted from perspiration.

We climbed aboard our swept-wing, twin turbojet Navy EA3B carrier aircraft which was scheduled to be our work station for the next four to five hours. Even with the portable air conditioner blowing cold air directly into the cockpit, the confined area would reach 120–130 degrees Fahrenheit before the crew and I could buckle on parachutes, survival revolvers and the safety harnesses in the aircraft seats. We hurried through our routines as quickly as possible after the portable air conditioner was moved away from the aircraft.

Rivulets of briny sweat cascaded down my forehead and across my face, stinging my eyes and blurring my vision of the runway there on the very edge of Subic Bay, Luzon.

We quickly completed the pre-start check list and brought both engines up to speed with their familiar, high-speed mechanical whine. A delightful blast of cold, dry air filled the cockpit as the pressurization system stabilized.

"Relief!" Jack grinned. All of us—my crew of six and I—thought the worst part of the day had passed.

We couldn't have been more mistaken!

I called Cubi Point Ground Control for taxi clearance, completed the pre take-off check list and waited for our take off clearance at the end of the runway. Everything looked "go" as we sat in our "office" where we would monitor and record enemy communications, radar, and fire control emissions during the next four of more hours of a routine flight.

NAS Cubi Point Control Tower responded to my takeoff request. "Navy jet seven niner six six, you are cleared for takeoff on Runway Niner. Wind zero eight zero at 10 knots. Turn left immediately after take off and come to a heading of two seven five degrees. Continue climbing en route to flight level three four zero. Maintain visual flight rules. Be advised of severe cumulonimbus build-ups on a line positioned north to south twenty miles west of Cubi Point. Cleared to en route frequencies. Good flight, Sir!"

"Wilco, Cubi Point Tower. Navy jet seven niner six six commencing takeoff now."

I firmly pushed the engine throttles forward all the way as I made a last second scan of the engine instruments. I released the brakes as the roaring turbojet engines reached full thrust. At just the correct instant on our takeoff acceleration schedule, I fired the aircraft JATO (jet assisted takeoff) bottles for additional thrust because of the high gross takeoff weight of our aircraft and the 116 degree F ambient runway air temperature. I was reassured by the steady, smooth JATO acceleration that increased our velocity as the runway raced beneath us and fell away behind.

No matter how many times an aviator who truly loves to fly experiences a take off, each one is exhilarating and delivers a spirit-lifting high of almost indescribable delight. It is then when you know the little boy in you is alive and well.

I reveled in the joy of piloting my 38 ton jet as it turned and climbed with effortless grace in, out, and around clouds west of Clarke Air Force Base and south of Mount Pinotubo. The aircraft responded instantly to my every command as it threaded its way between and around predicted giant columns of foreboding, turbulent cumulonimbus clouds.

We climbed rapidly to conserve fuel, ever-conscious that turbojet engines consume six to eight times as much fuel at sea level as they do at high altitudes with similar engine throttle settings.

The six men of this particular crew were magnificent, the best—well-trained, seasoned veterans, businesslike and professional. Each time we went airborne, they entrusted their lives to me, and I did not take their confidence lightly. I was proud to be their pilot. We shared precious mutual respect and flew as a well-coordinated team. Soon enough we would be over the Gulf of Tonkin near Hanoi.

My proud thoughts were interrupted by my navigator, Lt. Tim Demry.

"All the big bumps are behind us until we return," he said, peering into his radar scope. "I'm not making any rosy predictions about that line of thunder bumpers just west of Luzon. They could still be trouble on our way back."

Demry, in his late twenties, always had his nose in a book—not escape reading, but scientific and technical tomes. He was a superb athlete and enjoyed women but had vowed to stay single until he was once more a civilian.

I'd flown with Tim before and I respected his aware intuition that made him good at predicting weather problems. I tucked his cautious warning into the back of my mind.

We leveled off at 34,000 feet heading west out over the South China Sea. I maintained radio silence while monitoring my en route UHF/VHF frequencies. Post climb checklists completed, the crew settled in for the South China Sea transit. For the next one to two hours, we'd have radio silence and the crew had time to review check lists, emergency procedures, condition of reconnaissance equipment, and stowing of items not in use. They also had time to look inward.

Aerial reconnaissance missions into combat zones are paradoxical. They combine monotony and high stress—even moments of stark terror in some cases!

My first combat mission as a Navy pilot had taken me into the remote northwest corner of North Vietnam near Dien Bien Phu and close to the border of China. That first time, I was exhilarated with the new experience of being totally in harm's way, but that feeling quickly vanished.

I survived that to fly many dozens more and learned, early on, that missions in combat areas were dirty, ruthless hard work without promise of even one tomorrow. More dangerous than exciting.

Our mission on that day was generally uneventful, but it took longer than I had hoped.

The sun slipped below the western rim of Southeast Asia by the time we turned southward over Vinh. Jungle-shrouded mountains appeared beautiful and deceptively peaceful as they bathed in the alpenglow of the receding sunset. The Tonkin Gulf and all of Vietnam were rapidly covered in a cloak of haze and darkness.

My intentions had been to land at DaNang in South Vietnam for refueling, but as we approached, Jack Poss pointed to tell-tale bursts of explosives.

"Viet Cong mortar and rocket fire there, Commander," he said, "aimed at the field. Looks messy."

As the runway lights passed under the starboard wing of our aircraft, DaNang Control Tower warned, "All pilots, divert to alternate landing sites. Under attack here."

We wouldn't be refueling there.

Instinctively, I climbed to a higher altitude to conserve fuel. Luzon was about 700 miles away. I carefully checked and rechecked our fuel remaining. There were no aircraft carriers nor airborne tanker aircraft available for rapid refueling. Returning to NAS Cubi Point without refueling would be close, but it could be done. I could fly northwest across Vietnam and land at Korat Air Base, Thailand for refueling and limited ground support.

My aircraft, however, was in good enough condition to be turned right around to fly the next scheduled sortie if we returned to the Philippines before dawn. I felt certain that refueling at Korat airfield, with all the confusion and delays, plus an additional 800 miles of flight, would put our badly needed aircraft back at NAS Cubi Point too late to be used for the next scheduled mission.

The decision was mine:

We would return directly to home plate—NAS Cubi Point.

We set a course for Cubi Point, and I adjusted the throttles for maximum range fuel consumption. We would need every mile of distance I could squeeze out of each pound of JP-5 jet fuel that remained in our fuel tanks.

As we flew toward our distant Philippine destination, long chains of heat lightning performed crazy, erratic dances everywhere on the dark horizon. The crew was hushed as we continued eastward across the South China Sea. Each of us knew that the most hazardous part of our mission was yet to happen. I mentally reviewed severe weather emergency procedures in the silence of the darkened cockpit.

I instructed Jack Poss, my experienced aircraft captain, to secure the cockpit for a bumpy ride. Poss, with the help of Tim Demry and the other crew members, secured every piece of loose gear in the cockpit and living compartment aft where my four electronic technicians performed their highly classified monitoring and recording.

Poss grinned at me. "Sir, all items secured. We're ready for the rough ride if it happens."

All appropriate check lists were completed in the dim red glow from the cockpit instrument lights as our aircraft closed the distance to NAS Cubi Point at approximately seven miles a minute.

One hundred miles to go! My thoughts now focused on the ominous 60,000 foot high anvil-headed clouds that waited for us off the west coast of Luzon. As Demry had feared, they had increased in size and intensity since our take off. The thunderheads were clearly visible and were alive with lightning which silhouetted the angry gray and black cloud formations that hosted incredible, electrical energy, hail, heavy rain, and violent winds with vertical air currents.

No pilot would consider penetrating such weather if he had an alternate choice. My fuel gauges now indicated I was completely without options.

A hard knot tightened in my stomach as St. Elmo's fire began its blue lightning zig-zag across the cockpit windshield. I consciously ignored that distraction and radioed Cubi Point Approach Control for radar vectors to the runway. Radio reception was poor and garbled because of electrostatic interference, further complicated by nerve-shattering, earsplitting crashes of thunder generated by lightning bolts that shook our aircraft. The fuel gauges were dangerously low.

Two minutes to go before I would pull back the engine throttles and commence a low power descent beginning 75 miles west of the airfield. This trading of altitude for distance saved precious fuel for the final approach to the runway. Also, I would use some extra fuel on the way down to maintain flight control in the intermittent, violent turbulence that tossed our 26 ton aircraft about like a feather.

The hot air defrost was turned on "full hot defrost" to keep the frigid cockpit windshield—chilled by subzero high altitude temperatures—from freezing over with opaque frost when we plummeted into the warm, humid tropical air at lower altitude. I lowered my polarized sun visor over my eyes before turning on the white cockpit light to full intensity so I could still see the instruments while being partially blinded by the incredible intensity of nearby lightning flashes.

As we began our descent, a bolt of lightning struck the aircraft.

"We just lost our ASB-1 radar!" Demry said tensely. That was radar that helped us avoid severe thunder cells.

"No choice," I muttered. "We go according to plan." As we descended through 20,000 feet, I asked Demry to call out each 1000 foot increment of altitude as we passed through it. This was to keep me from flying right into the sea as I fought to maintain control of the aircraft while flying half blinded by lightning.

Any pilot needs a child-like faith in his flight instruments, particularly in instrument flight weather. In severe turbulence at night the arch enemy is vertigo!

But instruments don't get vertigo!

Pilots do!

My previous flight experiences in piloting hurricane hunting aircraft and penetrating severe hurricanes over the Caribbean Sea kicked in as we dropped into the black void in front of us. We passed through 13,000 feet in torrential rain and moderate turbulence. The aircraft took another lightning strike. The cockpit air temperature climbed as we descended into warmer tropical air and became painfully hot. With the defrost on full intensity the windscreen remained clear.

Cubi Point Approach Control crackled distantly.

"We've lost radar contact!" they sputtered.

The low fuel warning light glowed ominously in the lightning-illuminated cockpit. Torrential rain and turbulence pounded the aircraft.

"Continuing on our last heading," I advised Approach Control. It was our one chance to find and land on the runway.

"Seven thousand," Demry called out. "Six thousand. Five thousand."

I peered into the void.

Nothing.

"Four thousand!"

There it was! The string of runway lights grudgingly appeared out of the murky darkness and through blinding sheets of rain.

"Landing gear down! Wing flaps!"

Three miles later the view cleared. Our bird touched down on the rain-drenched runway centerline and decelerated through deep puddles and currents of rain water as we slowed to taxi speed.

Behind me, the crew roared and cheered out of sheer relief!

I taxied clear of the runway.

The cheers stopped. There was shocked silence.

The engines had shut down...completely out of fuel.

The passive aircraft with dead engines and stunned, silent crew was towed to the hanger.

We inspected our aircraft and discovered severe lightning scorching and many popped rivets, including two lightning strike holes big enough to push tennis balls through. But what a magnificent flying machine!

Before I departed the aircraft, I returned to the cockpit, turned on the power, and ran a thorough "fuel remaining" check. The fuel quantity system check indicated 1200 pounds of fuel remaining when both engines flamed out on the taxiway. We later learned that the fuel quantity system had malfunctioned. Had I needed to wave off and fly another pass to land, we would have crashed. Out of fuel!

Some skill. Some luck!

I silently thanked whatever gods that be, and I vowed to practice an even more stringent discipline of fuel conservation forever more!

I turned with Tim Demry to go to the flight line shack to fill out my yellow sheet history of the flight just completed.

There stood Poss and the back-end crewman, all smiles. "That was a great job, Commander," Poss said. "I speak for the whole crew. We would fly to hell and back with you in any kind of weather! But, Sir, please let me know before that flight, so the crew and I can add a couple of extra tons of fuel!" The other men broke in to boisterous laughter, and I heard a few exclamations of "Amen to that!"

I responded with a big grin, spun on my heel, and hurried to the flight line shack to fill out what I knew would be an extensive report on our just completed flight.

I mused as I wrote my report: "Where does the Navy get such men!"

None of my air crew slept well that night. The insufferable Philippine heat and humidity had little to do with it. I'm sure there were tortured dreams of empty tanks and malfunctioning gauges.

The following day, the seemingly endless war continued. My air crew and I flew back into the Gulf of Tonkin.

I was often recognized for my flying skill during the difficult years of flying for VQ-1 and SeaBrine. I received a total of 20 Air Medals similar to this certificate.

CHAPTER 18—

BUT FOR THE GRACE OF GOD:
Tet, 1965

Some of his entrails spilled out, red and ruptured through his torn belly.
A white rib gleamed evilly through his ripped chest.
The distinct cloying smell of fresh human blood
permeated the interior of the tent,
and I involuntarily gagged.

It was Tet, 1965.

Those of us who had been "in country" for a significant length of time or on a previous tour of duty were aware that all Hell would probably break loose after dark during the next three or four nights.

Tet is celebrated for three days beginning at the first new moon after January 20 each year. The North Vietnamese military and the Viet Cong guerrilla forces consecrated this holiday as a favorite time to kill and maim as many enemy military personnel as possible. They made extraordinary efforts to destroy our weapons and installations. Night became fearful hours when dark, malevolent bodies slithered in and unrelenting rockets rained down.

The DaNang Air Base bustled with apprehension. Supplies of small arms, machine guns, ammunition, grenades, rockets, and mortars were frantically relocated on the air base periphery based on observations of Viet Cong troop movement during that day. It was a giant chess game with desperate, fatal consequences for serious errors of judgment and timing. Sometimes a cruel twist of fate or a mindless chance determined the outcome of a man's life.

It had been a long, arduous, humid, tropical day—typically uncomfortable in February 1965. I closed out my third reconnaissance mission of the day by landing on the busy runway. I dreaded the humidity and torrid air temperatures that waited for my air crew and me as I taxied my EA3B electronic reconnaissance jet to the parking ramp. There I would turn off the cockpit air conditioning and shut down the turbo jet engines to reenter the grim reality of the earthbound.

My air crew and maintenance ground support personnel quickly refueled the aircraft while a tow tractor was being attached to the nose landing gear. Replenishment of LOX (liquid oxygen), engine oil, hydraulic fluid and any other consumables that were required would wait until the jet aircraft was safely tucked away in a revetment to protect the bird from damage or destruction from probable rocket and mortar attacks.

While those activities were being performed, my navigator, Lt. jg. Tom Knight and I coordinated and assembled all "gripes" (malfunction reports) to record on the maintenance yellow sheet (maintenance record of the flight with needed repairs). Any electrical, electronic, mechanical, and/or aerodynamic problems encountered in flight were also described in detail.

No air crew was allowed to depart the flight line and the aircraft just flown without preparing it as best they could for the next mission. This well thought-out procedure decreased the likelihood of an aircraft not being ready for taxi and takeoff in the event the airfield came under attack.

I was aware that chances were slim to none that I would be well-rested at dawn for the next 72 hours or longer. Trying to sleep while breathing stale air through mildewed mosquito netting had no romance at all! Coupled with that was the never-ending, disquieting high frequency of whirring wings of the ever-present, carnivorous, bloodsucking mosquitoes. Their whining search was for any minute breech in the netting to give access to human skin and blood. I eternally thanked and blessed the innovator/inventor of citronella candles. Thick repellent smoke from those candles did reduce the number of mosquito transfusions that I suffered—particularly while attempting to sleep. That was the good news.

The bad news was that candle light sometimes attracted the attention of snipers, and after I was shot at once, I always used a deep tin can as a container for the candle so the flame would not show.

My air crew and I completed preparing our aircraft for its next mission. We were tired, dehydrated, hungry, and wanted to shower as soon as we could return to our assigned quarters.

DaNang Air Base was burgeoning with its growing military population.

The United States Defense Department under orders of the President was sending great numbers of military personnel to many U. S. bases in Vietnam, including DaNang. The U. S. Air Force, the host armed service, was overwhelmed. They could not furnish enough living quarters or maintenance buildings.

The supply systems were jammed—saturated in a nightmare of over-abundance and logistics disorder. Often as not the supply system had procured badly needed parts and equipment that were incorrectly recorded in logistics inventories as to description, quantity, and/or storage location. It was not unusual to have aircraft and equipment listed as inoperable for lack of needed parts, only to discover days later that the desperately required supplies were, in fact, at DaNang. The parts simply could not be located in the confusion.

Such disarray was to be expected and anticipated. The overwhelming excess of arriving material was required to keep the ravenous war machine up and running 24 hours every day.

I was assigned to and encamped in temporary quarters in a large tent city with countless other U. S. officers from what seemed innumerable organizations. Maintenance personnel, pilots, and aircrew members from various Navy attack, fighter, and reconnaissance squadrons—along with transients who would only be at DaNang for short periods of time while waiting for transportation to other destinations—were all thrown together; people as jumbled and misplaced as supplies.

Most tent dwellers were intently focused on their own war assignments—too occupied to associate or fraternize with their neighbors caught up in a deadly time press with no opportunity or wish to socialize. The unvoiced consensus was that making too many friends increased the odds of suffering the grief and depression that followed daily fatalities.

Such was the way it was in Vietnam.

The huge sea of canvas covered dozens of acres. Tents sprawled over every available inch of the scrub fields near the airfield. Canvas V's fingered out from the central core like irregular tentacles of an oversized octopus. Tents were erected wherever stakes would support the poles in muck saturated by the incessant torrential rains. It was a veritable sea of canvas fully equipped with dark clouds of mosquitoes. Unending webs of tent ropes and stakes lay between these fragile shelters and the safety of the many centrally located bunkers. The thought of rushing through this maze toward safety in pitch black darkness with a hail of shells and rockets exploding nearby seemed hazardous—necessary, but appalling. The luck of the draw had situated me in a four man tent which was then unoccupied when I moved in—what luxury!

That evening—exhausted, hot, and apprehensive—I arrived at my assigned tent, anticipating privacy. As I threw back the tent flap, in the dim light I could see that my personal effects and bedding had been dumped unceremoniously onto an empty "rack" (bunk).

Indignation swelled.

A message had been contemptuously dropped on my belongings.

The terse note read, "I am Commander Klinefelter. I am assigned to this tent. I checked your date of rank. You are junior to me. I prefer your bunk. Your effects have been moved. RHIP (Rank Hath Its Privileges)

Viet Cong forces in the jungled area near DaNang Air Base made numerous rocket and mortar attacks. A well placed rocket took out the ammunition dump at DaNang. The concussion knocked down many wooden buildings for blocks around the explosions.

Though the note was accurate, it was provocative and undiplomatic. My Scottish blood pressure began to rise along with the hair on the back of my neck.

The bastard! Who did he think he was?

I looked outside. My tent partner was not in the vicinity. His absence bought me time to allow reason to prevail.

I decided a cold shower would be best. As the water beat down, I wondered: "Why had this Klinefelter felt compelled to commandeer my bunk when another unoccupied bottom bunk of equal quality, location, and desirability was available for his use? What kind of sick creature was this?"

Time gave me patience and perspective.

There was a war raging around us, and I could not let myself be distracted by such pettiness. My military duties and personal survival were my top priorities. Anything less would have to be ignored. I decided to overlook this dysfunctional conduct. My task was to stay alive!

After my evening meal and one very cold beer at the DOOM Club (DaNang Open Officers' Mess), I returned to my tent before sunset. My last precautionary act before entering my tent for the night was to again check my best route to the nearest bunker for shelter from the inevitable mortar and rocket attacks which always came during hours of total darkness and confusion. That taken care of, I entered my tent.

Commander Klinefelter was in a deep sleep as evidenced by the cacophony of his unpleasant snoring. He had decided not to bathe. He was wearing a filthy khaki flight suit, rank with grease spots, encrusted by salt, perspiration, and dirt. It was obvious that it had not been laundered in several days.

His prematurely balding head hung over the edge of the bunk like a floppy, grotesque doll. The few tufts of greasy brown hair remaining were glued against his sun-splotched scalp. Spittle oozed slowly from one corner of his gaping mouth. He was unshaven, unbathed, and he smelled like a horse that had been ridden hard and put away wet.

A half empty bottle of Johnnie Walker Red Label Scotch lay alongside his bunk.

I actually was relieved that he was unconscious so I could get some rest without useless discourse. I put my flak jacket, red-lensed flashlight, survival revolver, and my shoes next to my bunk. I tucked myself inside my mosquito netting and tried to sleep before the beginning of the inevitable rocket/mortar attacks, which, no doubt, would be forthcoming.

Obviously, I was very fatigued.

More than three hours passed before I awakened when incoming mortar rounds started exploding nearby. The Viet Cong had the range. They lobbed round after round into our tent city from the onset of the barrage. Fly-boys were prime targets. The Viet Cong were well aware that enemy aircraft did not deliver bombs, rockets, cannon fire and napalm without pilots and air crews.

The instant nearby explosions began, I jumped out of my bunk, put on my flak jacket, and pulled on my shoes. Grabbing all my carefully laid out gear, I hurried toward the bunker for a safe haven.

My progress stopped abruptly when in the blackness my foot caught a tent stake and the attached tent rope. My nocturnal reaction was simple and correct; I extended my arms in front of me to protect my face as I fell into the darkness, crashing into an area with numerous stakes and tent support ropes. Luckily, I did not impale myself on a stake as I tumbled down— sleepy, disoriented, frightened.

Immediately, I struggled to my feet, attempting to regain my equilibrium. The painful rope burns cleared my head of any sleepiness, and I was embarrassed, scared, and angry. Fortunately, my most severe injury was to my dignity after the awkward fall. One more moment and I entered the timbered, sand-bagged bunker, relieved to still be alive.

The bunker was pitch black, damp, crowded, and uncomfortable. It emitted the strong, offensive odor of marijuana smoke which was common in most of the American bunkers in country. I stumbled into darkness full of bodies and groped for a place to crouch. Red points of cigarettes glowed through the fetid blanket of smoke. An occasional murmur or the shifting of a body position betrayed the mute tension in the crowded blackness as we waited and listened for the next exploding shell—and the next after that.

The first attack lasted less than one hour.

My injuries from my fall smarted and burned, and I did not want another similar accident that night. Therefore, I decided to stay nearer to the bunker than my tent in the event the Cong decided to launch another attack before daylight.

I found a piece of tent canvas, and huddled under it against the side of the bunker away from the jungle in the humid discomfort, swatting mosquitoes, dreaming wistfully of my wife and daughter and the safety of Japan while I waited for the dawn.

There was a second attack about 3 a.m. of mercifully short duration. I suspected it was a torturous wake-up call to keep American servicemen from sleeping or getting decent rest before daylight—a deliberate scraping of already raw nerves.

Returning to my tent at first light, I observed that it had been riddled by shrapnel during the night attacks. When I looked up from within my tent, I saw the streaked pale dawn sky full of stars through the shredded top.

My plan was to eat breakfast, then shave before going to the flight line to ascertain possible aircraft damage. I hurriedly grabbed my shaving kit, and, as I turned to leave the vestiges of my tent, I glanced over at Klinefelter to see if he had recovered yet from his bout with King Alcohol.

I then realized that he had taken multiple hits of shrapnel in his chest and abdomen. Some of his entrails spilled out, red and ruptured through his torn belly. A white rib gleamed evilly through his ripped chest. The distinct, cloying smell of fresh human blood permeated the interior of the tent, and I involuntarily gagged. His eyes stared open wide in agony and terror, as if for one last moment he roused from his stupor to the realization and to his instant death in that black Tet night.

Normally, I would have been lying in the bunk that Klinefelter had commandeered from me.

There, but for the grace of God…

In the last analysis came the ultimate ironic twist. Some unknown person or persons removed the Klinefelter RHIP note from my bunk, obliterated the "H" from the RHIP, then taped the RIP to his dearly departed forehead.

The body had been removed when I returned after the day's reconnaissance flights. No witnesses were found nor did anyone come forward and admit to the note transfer. Naturally, I knew nothing, and to this day, I admit nothing.

Perhaps, at another time in another place Klinefelter and I might have shared a beer, talked, and learned to know and like one another. I'll never know.

However…Thank you, Commander Klinefelter, wherever you are.

CHAPTER 19—

TARGET FOR A SNIPER

The light of a citronella candle
Was all a sniper needed

The pup tents quickly gave place to wooden offices and barracks after the Tet Offensive, and, believe me, we were all relieved to get out of the discomfort and the mud.

As officer in charge of a detachment, I was assigned to a separate partitioned room in the barracks for officers. These barracks were designed for minimum exposure to sniper fire. This meant that the only open space for ventilation was immediately under the eaves along both sides of the building.

During the day, when I was not flying, I was in the maintenance officer's office or out inspecting personnel, or going from revetment to revetment checking maintenance on the aircraft.

The office was a dinky, dark hole in a hastily built structure, almost as unappealing as being in a broom closet. It was simply a tunnel to walk through. I would check my records and go elsewhere to do my paperwork as often as feasible.

One morning I was scheduled to fly and had been in the office. I needed to don a clean flight suit, so, instead of heading for the revetments, I aimed toward the officer's barracks.

I was less than 100 yards away from the office, when a V-C rocket made a lucky strike on the DaNang Airfield Munitions Dump.

The explosion was horrific. I didn't actually hear it, since the explosion was so loud that it temporarily totaled my ear drums. The force slammed me to the ground on my back and slid me through the gravel at least 10 feet with such force that it ripped holes in my shirt and plastered me with black mud. Not until much later did I realize that this had saved my life. Shrapnel flew over and around me, but since I was on the ground, I wasn't hit.

There were multiple explosions which flattened every building within several blocks. Men in the munitions area were killed or injured.

I staggered to my feet, stumbled toward the officers' barracks, and donned my clean flight suit after minor first aid on my back.

And took off on time for my scheduled flight!

I had two more day flights and a night flight, and it was not until off duty that I learned that the maintenance office was a shambles.

I was too busy fighting the war to put in for a Purple Heart. It seemed at the time that it was just another ho-hum day at Danang.

RIP to my maintenance office. The records were in the file cabinet in the foreground.

The officers' barracks were equally dangerous as I was to soon learn.

About a month after the explosion, I was ready to collapse in my bunk with its protective mosquito netting. The ventilation slots under the barracks eaves were no match for the hordes of mosquitoes that always found passage through the screens. That particular night, I had the somewhat unthinking notion that a citronella candle waxed to a jar lid would somehow repel at least some of the horde.

Now, citronella or "cymbogogon nardus," is extracted from a fragrant grass found in Southern Asia. This grass yields an oil used in perfumery and as an insect repellent. This was before the days of DEET, Cutter Repellent and other modern repellents and then was the only way to keep the whining critters at bay.

I lighted the candle, hoisted myself into an upper bunk and settled in for the night—I thought.

Zing! A sniper's bullet zipped through the external bulkhead of the barracks. I reflexively rolled out of the bunk five feet to the deck as a volley of shots penetrated the room just above my body. I jerked on the blanket and pulled the candle down and out.

We had an immediate meeting the next morning and I informed all hands of my sniper experience hours before. I ordered all hands that if they needed to use citronella candles to go to the mess hall and get empty cans deep enough to conceal the flame.

Sniping at the barracks happened after that, but there were no fatalities, since the snipers could shoot at a glow from a candle deep in an empty can, but not a specific target.

CHAPTER 20—

NO BUSINESS BEING THERE—
SPRING, 1966

"Grenade!" I yelled. The squad dived face down into the bush.
Instantly, small arms fire crackled all around us
as the incoming grenade exploded close to our left side.

I had no business being in the DMZ. I was not ordered to participate in any military covert action there. To this day, I'm not sure why I was there.

Spring of 1966 in Vietnam was normally hot, humid, insect infested and miserable. Most seasonal monsoons were past, but there was always rain, humidity, mildew, and boot-sucking black mud. Every variety of parasites in the world seemed to inhabit the land: lice, fleas, mosquitoes, all of which would feast on your flesh and transfer infectious microorganisms that caused anything from skin sores, blood poisoning, malaria, plague, typhus, and who knows what other exotic diseases.

During my many short deployments to Nam, I became acquainted with some very interesting service men—some of whom had special forces duties that regularly took them on hazardous assignments. I developed a peculiar bonding that unfolded gradually into special friendships with them, and we enjoyed each other's company when free time permitted.

They discovered that my Wisconsin childhood experience of living near large expanses of forested lands, and my love of hunting had served to make me an expert sharpshooter. They were happy to instruct me in the use of any weapons and small arms with which I was unfamiliar. My Special Forces friends often let me participate with them in practicing on a firing range, and we all enjoyed the competition, knowing well it was good "job insurance" for our line of business.

We had shared this rare and developing camaraderie for approximately a year as I flew into and out of the country. I always had many dozens of questions on their operations and procedures. They seemed to enjoy answering my questions and were very patient with their explanations. I, in turn, answered their multitudes of queries concerning jet flying and carrier air operations.

I sensed that my avid love of flying was contagious. It was intriguing for them and me to share first person stories of ground combat and wartime carrier air operations. We all learned from each other and gained great mutual respect.

They briefed me on booby traps, land mines, signs of ambush, punji sticks, hand signals, silent tracking, dirty tricks, trail marking, trip wires, camouflage, infiltration, and dozens of actions and reactions not used in hometown, USA. It was critical information that I soaked in like a blotter.

I was six again and playing at slaying dragons in the woods with my friends.

I was fascinated with punji stick traps because of their simplicity, easy availability and efficiency. They were devilish, ingenious holes dug into the earth deep enough for enemy combatants to step or fall into. The holes had many needle-sharp bamboo sticks installed points upward on which the unsuspecting victim would be impaled. Each bamboo needle was treated with agents to cause infection at the puncture point. One such commonly used substance was human feces because of its ready availability and its highly infectious nature.

These traps were installed on trails and footpaths which were probable foot traffic locations.

The traps were meticulously camouflaged but subtly identified so the Cong would not be trapped themselves. All that was needed to construct unlimited punji stick traps was a trench shovel and a sharp knife. Everything else was there in the bush in unending quantities. A victim of one of the traps would normally be out of combat action for months.

One man, a Special Forces sergeant named Griggs, briefed me on what could be expected out in "the bush." Griggs had the build of a well conditioned guerrilla fighter at 5' 10", and his demeanor left no doubt as to who was in charge. He was a leader of men who wore his immaculate uniform proudly. He had intense, penetrating brown eyes that pierced into your mind like a laser beam, invasively knifing through any inattention. I was a bit in awe of him.

One day, he quietly said to me: "No matter how knowledgeable and proficient you become in this kind of warfare, chances are—without some good luck—you will go home in a body bag—if they find your remains at all!"

It hit me in my gut like a hard fist. These same words fit carrier flying and flight deck operations. Officers and men who had trained and flown with me during most of my military career had said the same, and we had all seen luck deal out survival or death.

I had been flying missions to the north of DaNang for about 30 days and nights in March and April of 1966. Due to lack of aircraft spare parts and "up" aircraft ready for missions over North Vietnam, I had to wait for aircraft availability. When that occurred, I was scheduled to rotate back to my home squadron at NAS Atsugi, Japan. Once there, I knew I would be involved in reconnaissance flights off the seacoasts of Russia and North Korea across the Sea of Japan—not the best R & R after Vietnam, but inevitable.

Since I was marking time, I took the opportunity, early one morning to visit my Special Forces friends.

As soon as I walked into their bivouac area with all its temporary shelter and small one and two man tents, stacked arms, ammo cans and special equipment on wood pallets covered by canvas and camouflage ponchos, I sensed tension and a marked change of atmosphere. The strong odor of gun cleaning fluid penetrated my nostrils and further stimulated my curiosity.

As was usually the case, there were hundreds of wooden pallets stacked neatly along the perimeter of the bivouac area where they were guarded jealously. The empty pallets were precious for the soldiers and marines to install in their tents, storage areas, and walkways to elevate foot traffic above the gooey, staining mud that was ever-present.

Woe be to anyone who was caught trying to purloin pallets from neighboring military units. It almost always resulted in the guilty party getting the "stuff" kicked, knocked and beaten out of him. Justice was quick and severe.

The supply system personnel were forever complaining that thousands of pallets of battle supplies arrived in Nam daily and few, if any, empty pallets were ever turned in to supply.

An irate and frustrated, very senior supply commander once vented his ire in correspondence through his chain of command. The U.S. Marine "I" Corp Commander sent a response to the Air Force Supply Commander patiently explaining the urgent need to retain the empty pallets for morale, physical welfare and logistical requirements to keep military supplies dry and ready for combat use. He further placated the Air Force senior supply personnel by personally assuring the "I" Corp would return all wooden pallets to supply the first time it did not rain in Vietnam for one full fortnight.

The story goes as follows: the supply personnel have not received any pallets to the present day!

But, I digress.

My squad of friends were serious and businesslike. There was a dearth of conversation. Almost everyone was preoccupied with cleaning their weapons, packing their backpacks, checking munitions and special equipment. No one smiled. All movements were purposeful.

I took one of my friends aside and asked what was happening. He informed me that early that afternoon they were tasked to visit "Never-Never Land"—the Demilitarized Zone where neither side was supposed to be—and repair/replace certain equipment at a well hidden listening post, then return undetected to DaNang Air Base.

"That should be as easy as a task can get," the affable, sandy-haired Corporal McBride said, smiling at me through his suntanned, freckle covered face. He was to play a key role once the squad arrived at the listening post. He was a wiry, slightly built 150 pounder who had surprising strength and stamina. He easily carried as much or more than his share of equipment when in the bush. His forte was his thorough knowledge of electronic and infrared devices.

Griggs came in, his massive face darkly grim. "Sullivan just smashed himself up in a jeep," he said gloomily. The man had suffered a broken jaw in a head-on collision with a truck.

I knew Specialist Sullivan as a proficient auto/truck mechanic, the squad's transportation man, as Irish as a shillelagh, whose blond hair prompted a lot of good humored jesting about a Scandinavian who had sneaked into the Sullivan family tree. His loss to the mission was significant.

McBride looked me straight in the eyes, and chuckled. "Here's your free ticket to Never Never Land. How about it, Scott?"

"Are you serious?" I challenged McBride. "If not, say so now!"

Griggs turned his full, lasered attention on me. "You answered that without hesitation." His brow furrowed, and he paused. "Scott," he said, "I know you have been briefed thoroughly on the DMZ. You can break down weapons and reassemble them with the best of us. Every man in this squad knows you're an expert marksman and a sharpshooter."

The squad was silent. All of them watched the two of us.

My stomach tightened into a knot. Suddenly I knew the deadly serious implications of this hushed conversation and where it was leading.

A vision of my wife and six year old daughter raced through my frenzied thought processes. I could hear my father's voice reminding me, "Scott, know all your options. Review all your homework. Convert all odds to serve you as best you can!" My precious flying career could end right here, quickly, if I made the DMZ trek—no matter how it came out. Rational and irrational thoughts battled, cluttering my thinking processes.

Griggs' deep voice, vibrating like a heavy cello string, dropped further. "If you go with us and don't make it back, that would be it. We never heard of you—no trace—no record you ever existed. You'd just disappear." He paused again "Maybe it isn't such a good idea."

Specialist Jones was directly in front of me, down on one knee reassembling his weapon. His face was expressionless, but he was studying me for any sign of decision. He, like most of the squad, was in his early twenties, but he had a mature demeanor that belied his youth. A scar ran down his left cheekbone, testimony to a dare devil sledding accident from his teen years in Minnesota.

Wessel was about 6 feet 2 and muscular with wavy brown hair—a handsome dude. He smiled at me when he caught my eye and gave me his vote of confidence with a thumbs up hand signal.

Tibbs and Norton were both redheads and close friends. They were tasked to assist Corporal McBride with repair/replacement of electronic and infrared gear at the listening post. Tibbs, an auburn haired kid, claimed to be 20 years old, but his attempts at growing a mustache belied his assertions, and finally he had shaved it off. Norton, conversely, was an old man of 25 who could pass for 30. His light red hair was short cropped and curly.

The two had stopped packing gear, almost as if the moment were frozen time, and were watching me, an unstated, unblinking query. The other squad members were outside performing their logistic tasks.

I knew and trusted every man in the squad. These men were a giant step above most other Army personnel that I had encountered in Nam, educated and motivated...the best at their jobs...and my friends.

Subtle waves of nausea rippled through my stomach as I weighed the question.

"When do you need my decision?" I asked Griggs.

"Not later than 1030 hours. You'll need time after that to be equipped and briefed," he answered. "Think about it carefully."

I looked around, into the eyes of the men, one after another. They were still motionless, staring at me, studying my facial expression and waiting for my decision.

I had decided.

I wanted to go.

Worse, I needed to go, even if I couldn't have explained why.

To this day I can not explain why.

"If I go and return," I said in my most authoritative voice, "you each need to swear you never saw me. No record must show that I was there. Absolutely no information must get back to my squadron. I did not go—I was not there!"

Perhaps it was bravado. Perhaps it was to fill the silence.

We were toying with our careers—as well as our lives.

I would play by their rules. They would play by mine.

They nodded, almost imperceptibly.

I would go!

I had lunch before noon and was surprised that I had a good appetite. Time marched.

My visceral self operated at breakneck speed and excitement. Conflicting emotions vied for control of my thoughts and actions. From my flying experiences, I knew that once this military operation began, I would be too occupied to be concerned with trivial matters. The minor twinges of nausea were subsiding and the adrenaline pumped.

I called Griggs aside and said, "Sergeant, I'm leaving my rank south of the DMZ today. You're in command while we are in the bush." The subject did not come up again.

The squad and I wore camouflage clothing when we checked into the briefing area at 1300 hours. We carried dog tags but no other I.D.

Briefing over, we pre-positioned our squad at our start point; we locked and loaded weapons, checked ordnance, portable radios, compasses etc. and waited for our "go" time.

Our position was well away from DaNang City which had too many curious and prying eyes. We were sequestered in a well-secured location in an old abandoned cart path secreted in a waist high depression. A profusion of young bamboo and green scrub brush and tenuous vines had taken up squatters' rights along the hard-packed pathway. It was ideal to easily conceal ourselves there until we moved out to begin our clandestine operating.

We peered out of our hidden position at the edge of the depression. Vietnamese women passed by, unseeing in their backbreaking work, their harshly sun-shriveled faces, deeply carved with wrinkles, their eyes blank and unseeing, their days of forthcoming senectitude guaranteed by their daily, unending, monotonous bending and stooping in the muddy rice paddies. Their figures bobbed like toys: conical wide straw hats, silhouetted black cotton shirts and pants, dark stained feet and lower legs. None of them wore shoes in the wet, muddy paddies.

There was constant planting and harvesting of rice anywhere fresh water could be retained by mud paddies and dikes. Every square foot of land available—any shape, size, or quantity—was utilized for rice or other food production.

"H" hour came. We quickly moved northward out across low land and rice paddies filled with rice plants inundated with water and dark brown to black mud. The low elevations soon gave way toward higher ground into "Never-Never" land.

Heavy stands of ever present bamboo, incredible cover for ambush, impeded our progress in most directions. Corporal McBride snaked directly in front of me as our column moved as quietly as possible through shoulder-tall thick foliage—and sometimes painful—sharp saw grass. We communicated by hand signals. Four of us carried listening post repair parts in addition to our regular weapons and equipment. Periodically we were relieved of the heavy repair parts by others in our ten man squad.

Suddenly, Griggs hand signaled, "Halt." He beckoned me forward and pointed out a cleverly disguised trip wire that had been set by a cunning enemy for unwary Americans. My untrained eyes would not have detected it.

It was a great lesson for me, and I knew that Griggs had just saved my life. I would thank him later.

We changed our trail away from the trip wire area, circumnavigating through heavy bamboo and waist-to-shoulder high, verdant, tall grass and scrub brush. Griggs paused briefly to scribble a note for the debriefing team about the trip wire. We left it armed as we found it. No need to announce our position with unnecessary noise.

We approached the listening post. Though I had been pre-briefed, I was surprised at the relative nearness of the listening post to the southern border of the DMZ. We were approaching the listening post generally from the south, but with dozens of course changes to avoid suspicious areas, impenetrable bamboo and brush, defoliated areas, and to remain out of highly visible locations. Such maneuvering made our terrestrial navigation difficult and inaccurate at best.

My best estimate of our distance traveled north into the DMZ was approximately a mile and a half.

We were getting close to our destination. Sergeant Griggs transmitted a short coded radio message to home base giving our position.

In the delay, I took a stingy sip of fresh water from my precious, limited supply, aware of the sage, cautionary advice to conserve every possible drop.

It seemed logical and practical that establishing more northerly listening posts would have little value for the U. S. Military. There was no point in risking fire fights and significant fatalities by placing the posts along the northern DMZ border. The enemy was no real threat unless they came within one or two miles of the southern DMZ border as they invariably did during each annual Tet season. They killed as many American military personnel, destroyed as much military equipment, and damaged as many installations as possible. The attacks were always nocturnal armed forays into South Vietnam out of the DMZ.

The post was in a narrow north-south valley. The Cong, trespassers from the north, used the gentle slopes and contours as an easy thoroughfare, avoiding the impenetrable stands of bamboo on each side of the valley. I was truly impressed at how artfully the Special Forces men had established the listening post.

McBride and his two specialists, Tibbs and Norton, cautiously entered the listening post area, avoiding their own preset booby traps and inspecting everywhere in case the Viet Cong had discovered the post and added their own treacherous traps, so that we would have become the hunted instead of the hunters.

The freckled McBride and the two red heads were out of sight, but we knew exactly what the three men were doing from photographs of the post's interior which we had examined during the mission briefing. No piece of man made equipment was visible in the post. It was all perfectly disguised in natural vegetation, rocks, and earth contours.

McBride and the two others worked quickly to make repairs, adjustments and replace power packs as needed. Griggs deployed the remaining squad members to provide security.

The two expert squad personnel, who had been briefed before the mission, gathered selective pieces of foliage to eliminate traces of our visit. They constructed crude but effective rakes from scrub brush to hide traces of ingress/egress foot paths from our post. They removed and hid broken foliage, twigs, crushed plants and branches—a masterful job.

The squad quickly reformed and left the scene—undetected. We had successfully performed our assigned task and were on our way back.

"That should be as easy as a task can get," McBride had commented.

We purposely returned by a circuitous route to foil enemy tracking, easy enough because of the dense vegetation. We had moved approximately 500 yards from the listening post and I felt that we were home free for the first time since we entered this never-never land.

One heartbeat later, out of the corner of my eye, I saw a hand grenade lazily drifting down toward the squad. It appeared as in slow motion and descended in an arc toward us.

"Grenade!" I yelled.

The squad dove face down into the bush.

Instantly, small arms fire crackled all around us as the incoming grenade exploded close to our left side.

I lobbed a grenade back in the direction from which the first grenade had arrived. It exploded just as it was entering the foliage. A concussion sounded, followed by shrieks of pain.

I was too occupied to realize how frightened I was. All I felt was anger—glowing, fierce hatred at someone who was trying to kill me and my friends.

Just as in harrowing danger situations as a pilot, I found myself calm and calculating. I slithered about ten yards on my stomach, ten yards away from the previous grenade explosions and toward the safety of nearby bamboo bushes.

I found myself close to two squad members who had been severely wounded by gunfire and grenades.

Far worse, when I got to them to render aid, I realized their wounds were fatal. One of the dead was Norton. I recognized his pale, curly red hair. He had taken several rounds of bullets through his chest. The other man I could not recognize. Too much of his face was missing. I stripped off their dog tags, ammo, hand grenades and water canteens and crawled away from the cadavers, because grenades were still exploding nearby.

The extra grenades were a premium. I returned grenade for each grenade when I could determine the incoming trajectory.

Jones dived into my bamboo cover, thankful for the shelter from the small arms fire. He had a few minor shrapnel wounds that could wait until we got out of the danger area. The scar on his cheek was white and stretched.

He grinned crookedly, "Thanks for the hospitality, Sir."

"Welcome aboard, Jones. Start firing NOW!" I retorted.

He did, and with vengeance.

The tide of combat had shifted. We had better weapons, more grenades, and a mortar launcher with about a dozen mortar shells. Within ten minutes the small arms fire decreased to a sniper-like staccato. The squad was unaware that the ambush had broken off and the Cong had melted into the shadowed brush. They probably were concerned that American reinforcements would arrive, since we were approaching the southern border of the DMZ.

McBride dashed toward the heavy bamboo cover in which we two were concealed.

There was a familiar sickening thud—a bullet hitting flesh. McBride pitched forward with blood gushing from his belly.

I grabbed his arm and in one giant tug, he was with me in the temporary safety.

I ripped open his clothing.

There was one clean gut shot through his midsection that had missed his spine. Like many gunshot wounds, the slug had entered his back small and exited his midsection larger and uglier. He was hemorrhaging profusely. His freckled face was blanched. I worked feverishly to stem the heavy flow of blood, using my first aid kit and his. I sterilized his wound, stuffed the gaping, angry hole in his abdomen with sterile gauze pads, and taped him shut as well as I could.

Bullets tore through the bamboo stems and tattered the leaves. I was relieved that he was unconscious. His abdomen was a gory mess; the pain would have been excruciatingly unbearable.

I was swearing to myself as I worked: "Just give me one clean shot at that bastard! I'll take him out so fast!"

I removed all unnecessary weight from the comatose McBride. Jones said he would stick with me and give me cover while I attempted to carry and drag McBride out of the hell we were in.

The Viet shooter who had the three of us pinned down in the bamboo with small arms fire finally made the mistake I was waiting for. I caught a fleeting glimpse of his movement through the foliage.

I saturated the heavy vegetation, laying five or six rounds into his location in about three seconds. I could not be certain I had him, but the small arms fire stopped immediately and did not resume.

I threw McBride over my shoulders, half-carrying, half-dragging him, with Jones covering our retreat. Another member of the squad overtook McBride and me. It was Tibbs, the teenager with the shaved mustache, a good friend and assistant to McBride. He wanted to help carry his friend, and I was fortunate that he came when he did.

I had become aware for the first time of a severe pain in my thigh. In the excitement of the fire-fight, I had not realized that I had taken a small piece of shrapnel in my leg, but carrying McBride had exacerbated the problem.

No one could later understand how I dragged, pulled, tugged, and carried McBride almost a mile out of the ambush. I am not certain either, but this I know—I have a terrific adrenaline pump—and I was totally scared!

The squad lost three good fighting men that spring day in 1966 during a fire fight in the DMZ. They were men who lacked the "good luck" that Sergeant Griggs said all men needed. Only their dog tags came home that day

I inquired why we had not received any air support.

"Shit!" Wessel, the handsome dude, said, "The first shots hit our damned radio and blew it all to hell!? No radio—no air support!"

When we got back to our base camp, Griggs shook my hand and saluted. "Commander," he said, "I would confidently march into Hell's gate by your side, knowing I could rely on you completely…"

I didn't feel brave; just relieved and grateful to be back.

I said my farewells to the squad. It was like leaving family. We were all subdued and mourning, each in our own way. We had become as one.

My last cautionary words to them were, "I did not go. I was not there."

They nodded, understanding my situation. We needed to say no more.

A medic taped up my minor wound. He asked no questions, just repaired the damage. "Sure is deep in there," he said and pulled out a one inch metal splinter from my gluteus muscle.

My next deployment to DaNang Air Base was May, 1966, more than a month later. I found Griggs, who told me that the remains of the three men had been re-covered by helo the day after the fire fight.

"McBride beat all the odds," he grinned. "Thanks to great medics, an expeditious helo-medivac, and outstanding O.R. surgeons, and some anonymous Navy guy who just happened to be there and carried him out of hell, McBride survived! He's home in the U.S. and recovering satisfactorily. Great news!"

Griggs said he could put me in for an official Purple Heart after this episode, but I had more sense than that. The group, half kiddingly, presented me with an unofficial Purple Heart and a Bronze star which I treasure to this day.

But at the time what good would it have been to have had an official Purple Heart and a court martial!

CHAPTER 21—

ALPHA ATTACK

We were the watch dogs of the sky;
Sometimes helpless canaries in the mine.
Our task was to give pilots an edge when the deadly SAM's whistled
upward.

I hope I can be forgiven.

When the anti-aircraft exploded on our starboard side, I think the impact and the shock wiped away some of my memory.

I have heard that others who have been in auto accidents can remember bits and pieces…or nothing of the actual event, so I cling to the notion that that explains the haziness of my memory.

Also, each day might bring a different set of crew members. There was no one navigator or flight engineer, but only the one assigned for the day.

I can't remember the day, the season, or the year. Nor can I remember the name of my excellent navigator who was strapped in beside me and felt the brunt of the North Vietnamese angry reaction. Yet the events of that day cause me to quiver with excitement, to raise my voice in disgust, and to want to strike out at the unnamed meddling U. S. politicians that tied our hands

It was a routine Alpha strike, something which happened two or three times a week when I was stationed in DaNang.

Alpha strikes were used when it was needed to dump on a single target complex in a short period of time or it was necessary to penetrate very heavy defenses, such as in attacks near Haiphong or Hanoi. All available aircraft on the carriers in the Tonkin Gulf became a single strike group. Alpha strikes were usually coordinated with aircraft from other carriers on the line and often with U.S. Air Force strike efforts coming out of Thailand. If five carriers were on line, as many as five Alpha strikes could pound a single target within an hour.

Before an Alpha strike, air operations were suspended for two hours prior to launch time to allow all aircraft to be refueled, rearmed, and spotted for the launch. After the strike, it took up to an hour and a half to resume cyclic operations which could then continue for the rest of the day or night.

In an Alpha strike, U. S. forces combined their massive resources and strength to saturate the enemy territory with napalm, rockets, missiles…anything and everything available. The point was to take out strategic military targets—bridges, weapon sites, anti-aircraft guns, and SAM's (Surface to Air Missiles), when they could be found. All Navy attack aircraft were there, along side all the Air Force aircraft available. Each bomber pilot had his launching order and his priority targets as a part of the intricate web of explosions that would fill the sky.

The VQ-1 task, in this case my job, was to fly off to the side of the attack aircraft but close enough for excellent electronic surveillance. The "spooks" who monitored the equipment on my trusty EA3B would read the enemy's Fire Control radar signals and tell me on the ICS (Inter Communication System) within the aircraft that a SAM had been fired.

I, in turn, would call the code word on the "Guard" channel to warn the attack pilots that a missile was headed in their direction. Then, if the pilot was observant, had quick reaction time, was skillful—and lucky—he could avoid the SAM and make the missile self destruct.

I flew off a carrier, and again, I can't sort out which carrier it was, because these flights happened so often and so many carriers were used, that memory fails. There would be one and sometimes two carriers in the Gulf of Tonkin as a part of the Alpha strike. Afterward, they would often steam out of the Gulf, away from the range of land based armament. Other aircraft came from safe land bases, from Thailand as well as South Vietnam.

Early in the morning, I would go to the Ready Room where the many pilots assembled. I would have been informed by a coded message sent from ship to ship and to the many land bases as to the critical code word for the day—always a one syllable, easily understood word.

The list of daily code words was often changed: at first every two to three weeks, later every week or less. When there were two or three Alpha strikes in a day, there would be alternate code words.

If pilots heard me say that code word, it would give them a warning that might be the difference between life and death.

Perhaps the word for the day would be "Blue." When we were all aloft, and my "spooks" spotted a SAM headed for the attack aircraft, I would clearly state: "Code Blue. This is Code Blue!" This would be transmitted on the "Guard" channel that overrode all other communications, so that every pilot heard it clearly.

The pilot would then scan below and behind him for the tell-tale "white telephone pole," and if he saw it homing in on his aircraft, he would ready himself. Just as the missile came within striking distance, he would make a 6 "g" turn, sharply upward starboard or port. If he did it right, the missile would try to follow and destroy its inner guidance systems and/or its control surfaces while attempting to follow and then would spin harmlessly out of control to the ground.

Not all pilots were that skillful or lucky. We lost many men that way. All I could do was give them the edge.

We had finished our run for the day and were headed back toward DaNang. I had called the code word out several times that day.

We were near Vihn at 23,000 feet when an anti-aircraft shell exploded near the starboard side and severely damaged the cockpit.

We instantly lost pressurization and I immediately put my aircraft in a steep dive toward a low altitude as we all grabbed for our oxygen masks.

There was blood everywhere, on the windshield and all over my body.

I thought at first I had been hit, though I felt no pain, but I was so busy those first minutes that I did not realize that it was my navigator.

When I slapped on my oxygen mask, I tasted blood in my mouth and thought it was my own.

However, the blood was from my navigator. His upper right leg had been shredded by the shrapnel. I had to wipe the blood from my helmet to see that he was slumped unconscious in his seat.

We lost our port engine when we lost the ATM (Air Turbine Motor) that pressurized the cockpit. Then the port engine caught fire. We lost the hydraulic pump and hydraulic boost to the flight controls—a major electrical failure.

I was much too occupied trying to save our aircraft and our lives to help my navigator,

The flight engineer, who had minor wounds himself, unstrapped himself, came forward at my direction, unstrapped the navigator and put him on the cockpit floor between my seat and the navigator's. He administered first aid, wrapping the leg, tourniquet style, to quench the flow of blood.

He too was in shock from the explosive decompression. It was not until he returned to his seat, that he realized he had been wounded. That engineer no doubt saved our navigator's life.

I gave the crew the option of bailing out and told them I would stay with the aircraft and the navigator, no matter what.

In unison, the crew opted to remain with the aircraft as long as I could keep it airborne.

I headed the smoking aircraft in the direction of DaNang 230 miles southeast over enemy territory and limped in on one engine.

The medics hurried my navigator away, and he survived with a Purple Heart.

I still must apologize that his name escapes me but I can see him in my mind's eye and know that it should never have happened.

This EA3B held a crew of seven when we were damaged by a near miss anti-aircraft explosion at 23,000 feet over Vihn, Vietnam. The navigator sat at the upper impact point. I was lucky to be on the port side, away from the impact. Had I not been, none of us would have survived.

The problem with the War in Vietnam was that the meddling politicians in Washington, D.C. by some means had usurped command control from the senior generals and the admirals. Major, important targets had been designated as "off limits" by the powers that be. Bombers could attack the smaller targets and had to spare the important ones. It was by edict from Washington. It makes no more sense to me now than it did then, but if many of the targets had been taken out as all the fly-boys and their superiors wanted, there might have been fewer operative anti-aircraft guns to injure my navigator.

I served my country and was proud that I was a warrior, but I will always question the wisdom of those who did not let us win.

My accolades go not to them, but to the men and women who served in all the carrier task groups, those with whom I went down to sea during my Navy flying career.

They are the thousands of personnel in the carrier task groups who are the muscle and backbone. They provide the technology, expertise and hard labor that always put the jet pilot into the skies in immaculately maintained aircraft. These are the extraordinarily dedicated people who deserve the highest praise for their professionalism and patriotism. It is as true today as it was then

I will always believe that these air task group personnel were an integral part of my success as a Navy carrier pilot and deserve the highest praise for keeping the pilots and aircraft fit to protect the very ramparts of our great nation. Since the genesis of carrier aviation, they have always been the best of the best.

CHAPTER 22—

OVER A BLACK SEA—JULY, 1967

"Commander!" Bill shouted excitedly over the intercom,
Four Chinese fighters are taxiing for take off from Hainan Island!"
I had no desire to wait around to learn their intentions.

My air crew and I finished our evening preflight brief—another probably boring, routine night reconnaissance with our yawning faces reflected in sky darkened windows and minds occupied with charts, radar, and things unseen on the ground and ocean below. Our mission was to carefully record both search and fire control radar locations and electronic signatures, as well as SAM (surface to air missile) sites.

Night reconnaissance flights were flown in a darkened aircraft dimly illuminated by the red flight instrument lights in the cockpit and lights of special security equipment aft of the cockpit. Air crewmen who had flown earlier day flights and those who slept poorly because of the mortar attacks the previous night were prone to doze off. One of the insidious, chronic problems that always arose on that kind of flight was complacency. Monotonous routine and repetition were usual.

Sometimes, however, something out of the ordinary would occur.

The potential danger was that boredom could dull the acute awareness an air crew needed. Without that alert awareness, one critical oversight could spell disaster. That, we all knew, yet night after night of such flights could lull us into that dangerous complacency.

It had been an uncomfortable torrid July day in 1967, normal enough for Vietnam. "Expected" or not, I never truly acclimated to the local weather conditions and climate. There were never-ending irritants to remind us we were living in hell on earth—diseases, heat rash, infections that would not heal for seemingly interminable periods of time, poisonous snakes, spiders, scorpions, centipedes, roaches, leeches, flies, fleas, and never-ending mosquitoes.

I put all that behind me as I commenced our takeoff roll from DaNang Air Base. Climbing at full thrust, I turned northeastward to go feet wet (over water) as our EA3B turbojet aircraft continued our ascent over the Tonkin Gulf east of Vietnam and west of Hainan Island, China. I changed our climb out heading to parallel the Vietnamese coastline and remained well clear of China.

As always, we immediately completed our post take off check list to ascertain that our bird was up and ready for our mission. We leveled off at flight level Two-Five-Zero (25,000 feet) in a matter of minutes. The air crew commenced their mission tasks during climb out and Lt. Tom Wilson, my navigator, and I verified and concurred on the track we were flying.

We had no intention of inadvertently straying into Chinese air space—a sometimes fatal error.

Tom and I both relaxed a bit as our ASB-1 radar and other navigational aids verified that all was quiet on the Chinese fighter base at Lingshui Airfield on Hainan Island as we passed it well east on the starboard side of our craft.

"I always check," Tom said, "and double check our track west of that base so we won't stir up a hornets' nest!"

"Amen to that," I concurred.

We were both quiet, thinking the same thoughts. We both knew that if the Chi Com fighters climbed out of Lingshui after us, they'd be aiming for a kill, and as an unarmed reconnaissance aircraft without fighter escort, we also knew we were "dead meat" if the ChiComs wanted it to happen.

Tom and I were fully aware that it would not matter which party was in the right, even if we were in our legitimate airspace. The ChiComs were infamous for shooting first and then lying impassively after the shoot down.

I had a technician—Bill Sanders—aboard who spoke and understood conversational Chinese. I had instructed him prior to take off during our briefing to closely monitor any and all ChiCom (Chinese Communist) tactical air radio frequencies. He was to keep me apprised real time of any pertinent messages that might in any way affect our flight.

An hour into our mission, we were abruptly shaken from any complacency.

"Commander!" Bill shouted excitedly over the intercom, "Four fighters are taxiing for take off from Hainan Island!"

We checked their assigned climb out vectors, and bells rang in my head. It seemed clear they had ugly intentions toward our aircraft before we could return to DaNang Air Base just south of the DMZ (demilitarized zone).

Of course, the ChiComs possibly were unconcerned whether I had entered their airspace. They may have been only intent on shooting down an unarmed U. S. reconnaissance jet aircraft since they were infamous for fabricating webs of lies as to who had violated whose airspace and did what to whom.

I had no desire to wait around to learn their intentions.

We were cruising at above flight level Two-Five-Zero to reduce probable SAM missile launches at us at that altitude and slant range.

I immediately extinguished all aircraft exterior lights, went to full thrust, reversed course, and continued to climb. I wanted extra altitude to convert to additional airspeed if a deadly race to intercept got underway. Every minute would be precious to close on DaNang Air Base. If we needed maximum speed for a run for home plate in DaNang, I wanted to be sure we had it. I had to get that altitude while the supersonic fighters were still taking off and rendezvousing. My plan was to maintain maximum altitude and airspeed all the way south. That would force the ChiCom fighters to consume maximum fuel during their climb to intercept.

I passed over the fighters' positions at my maximum, level subsonic air speed while the interceptors were still climbing to my altitude.

The Chinese fighters had supersonic flight on their side. My aircraft could not break through the sound barrier. It was limited to just over .9 Mach.

"The fighters have been ordered to turn southward," Sanders told me in a quietly warning voice.

I knew at that moment that my only choice was to assume the ugly worst and run like hell!

My crew worked in tense silence as they stored all loose gear in anticipation of possible high "g" maneuvering. I set the canopy defrost air to full-hot manual in anticipation of the forthcoming power glide that would rapidly take us out of the high altitude subzero temperatures and inject our aircraft into the hot, humid atmosphere near the Earth's surface. There was no way that I wanted the aircraft cockpit canopy to completely frost opaque. We would have no chance of evading the fighters or surviving a missile shoot if I couldn't see where we were going.

We leveled off at approximately FL 340 (altitude 34,000 ft.) and continued accelerating with throttles at full thrust. I knew that would be all the altitude we needed, based on our maximum speed requirements vs. our .9 plus Mach power glide if that became necessary.

I ordered my crew to check their parachutes and survival equipment for possible bailout.

The men were dead quiet. They knew what was at stake.

The ChiComs had guns and missiles; we had none! I knew I had to muddle this intercept any way I could.

I retrimmed the aircraft for a maximum speed power glide.

I squawked "EMERGENCY" on my IFF (identification friend or foe) transmitter and transmitted "MAYDAY" on the UHF guard radio frequency, calling to any U. S. fighter aircraft in our vicinity to intercept the ChiCom fighters and to take care of business! I was fairly certain there were no friendly fighters in the vicinity, but the ChiComs did not know that. Let them be distracted.

The deadly race was on.

The odds were against us if the fighters had been ordered to shoot us down. The lives of my crew were in my hands.

The ChiCom fighters were now beginning to close on my aircraft from below at my 6 o'clock position. I punched over into a maximum speed full power glide and descended fast enough to keep my airspeed near .9 Mach. The frame of my subsonic aircraft vibrated violently from sonic shock waves generated on the wing and empennage (tail) control surfaces. I was pushing that baby beyond her capacities. All the hundreds of hours of training for low level atomic delivery kicked in, and my actions became almost automatic

I reluctantly decreased speed a few knots to improve stability and controllability but continued the screaming dive toward the pitch black waters of the Tonkin Gulf. I'd give those fighter pilots plenty of distractions to make any missile shots difficult and as inaccurate as possible—or better still—I'd entice them to crash into the Tonkin.

"The fighters have received orders to follow us down, Sir." Bill Sander's voice was tight.

I increased our aircraft dive angle until the controls felt like they were about to rip off our aircraft. Getting down to sea level without disintegration became my first priority. I throttled back to use less engine thrust and increased our dive angle further to reduce the time needed to reach sea level while dampening the sonic wave vibration.

My navigator, Tom Wilson, gave a running dialogue of each 1,000 feet of descent at our more than a mile-a-minute dive. It was our life insurance to keep me—the extremely occupied pilot—from flying right into the invisible, enveloping black, unforgiving salt water just below us.

We passed the last thousand feet of altitude. Our vertical descent accelerated...

Tom shouted out: "One thousand! 900! 700! 500! 300!?

Still no missile explosions!

My oxygen mask nearly ripped off my face from the high "g" forces resulting from our recovery from our dive. My hundreds of hours flying below 50 feet of altitude as a conventional aircraft atomic delivery pilot trained to avoid radar detection would now pay dividends. Our best chance—perhaps our only chance—was to skim the surface of the water. I didn't have to be concerned with terrain avoidance, but the fighters would—if I crowded the Viet shoreline!

I reasoned that they would also be concerned about possible U. S. fighter intercept.

They knew we could not out speed them. But I could give them an experience that was no part of their fighter training. They would have to chase and strike a low level target in total darkness at blazing speed on the surface where no radar assistance could reach them from Hainan Island.

I needed that edge.

I added thrust and leveled off at 200 feet above the black sea and decelerated to 550 knots at near full thrust with no more altitude to convert to airspeed. I adjusted my elevator trim to provide just enough nose up trim to make me consciously work at remaining below 150 feet.

I couldn't allow an iota of nose down trim to cause loss of altitude. At approximately 625 miles per hour, a second of nose down trim could have ruined the entire flight!

A check of the radio altimeter showed it functioning normally. That gave me a more accurate measurement of low altitudes than did the pressure altimeter. I gradually coaxed our bird down to 100 feet.

Tom had a good functioning ASB-1 radar and gave me headings to keep our aircraft "feet wet" approximately one mile offshore. My crew knew we were not going "feet dry" over land, but the fighter pilots did not know that. Terrain avoidance would give them a serious distraction to muck up their possible missile shoot if there was one intended.

No missile shots yet—a very good sign! We could not out speed them, but I would give them plenty distractions to ruin their concentration. We were no longer certain that the fighters were still with us, but I was not going to pull up and make a bull's eye for a missile.

I climbed to 150 feet and made a very cautious, shallow course correction toward DaNang, so I wouldn't drag a wing tip in the water. Several dozen dim, white masthead lights of fishing boats flashed by and below us in a streaked blur of speed as we passed the DMZ and generally headed toward DaNang Air Base.

For the first time since the deadly pursuit began, though still over water, I truly felt we had a chance to make it back safely. We approached DaNang at breakneck speed, still very low. I pulled back my throttles, opened my speed brakes, pulled up from the salt water surface into a momentary 4 G climb, quickly rolled starboard to an almost inverted attitude while dissipating my excess airspeed without further climb.

At some point before the maneuver, the fighters had given up the chase, turned tail, and retreated toward their own safety of Hainan Island. We completed our landing check list and landed uneventfully. As we taxied into our assigned revetment for parking, my hands trembled a bit.

When I shut down the engines, the disciplined, silent crew suddenly burst into speech and slapped each others shoulders, laughing more when they discovered that all were soaking wet from nervous perspiration. Our wild, hair-raising commute was finished.

Exactly when the ChiComs broke off the pursuit or why was never clear. We knew from the intercepted tactical radio messages that they had followed us down to the surface of the sea. Evidently they were none too enthused about the high stakes, high speed, very low altitude pursuit on a black night after a target that skimmed above fishing boats in a wild commute. There were so many variables at work during the pursuit that we will never know why we escaped what could have been an easy shoot down.

I had chosen to flee. It was a logical decision for me at the time, with six fine crewmen my responsibility, I was not going to give up. I would risk such a flight to keep us all alive. The air crew unanimously—with boisterous relief—agreed that we didn't need another mission like that one—ever again. We were all painfully aware, though, that our destiny was not ours to control.

We would be sent out again.

ChiCom fighters could spot and pursue us again. If we were ordered out, we would go. That aircrew was comprised of loyal, brave, dedicated men! It was an honor to pilot such people out of harm's way.

Shortly after securing our aircraft, a 1st Marine messenger requested that I report immediately to the 1st Marine Air Intelligence Officer for a very thorough and professional debriefing. Any unusual happenings were subject to the "I" Corps Intelligence group and would be added to their data collection.

Before getting into the messenger's jeep, I called my crew together. "Tonight," I told them, "you earned your flight pay! I am so proud of your performance under such stressful survival conditions. I'm proud to fly with you."

My navigator, Tom Wilson, put his hand on the jeep. "Scott," he laughed, "you pulled some great maneuvers out of your hat tonight. Where in Hell did you learn all that?"

"Believe me," I responded, "it was extemporaneous. I was just sitting in the cockpit next to you with nothing to do, so I contrived a couple of stunts to entertain the ChiCom pukes"

Tom and the others doubled over with laughter as the messenger drove me off in the jeep.

My flip answer disguised my actual condition.

A medicinal drink at the DOOM Club (DaNang Open Officers' Mess) was inadequate to bring me down enough to sleep amid the mosquitoes and the occasional rocket/mortar attacks in the humid, sweltering heat. A second round and a refreshing shower, however, worked just fine.

I was totally exhausted. I barely managed to stay awake long enough to offer a silent prayer of thanks to my Super Being who rode with my crew and me at less than 100 feet and 625 mph above the black maelstrom of Tonkin Gulf.

I arose in the morning to fly my next recon mission at dawn.

The way it was.

CHAPTER 23—

THE WAY IT WAS:
SEPTEMBER, 1967

As the chopper hovered there, we could see a saffron-robed object dropping toward the concrete runway.
As it splattered at impact, we saw clearly that it had been a human.

It had rained torrents before dawn, but a beautiful autumn sunrise glimmered over the South China Sea east of DaNang, South Vietnam. The intermittent nocturnal rains had lowered the ambient temperature to the high eighties, and the relative humidity was about 87% but climbing on that comfortable September morning in 1967.

Those of us who had been "in-country" for some time knew that a day without sweat, fatigue, gunfire, and death was very unlikely. We grasped eagerly at such rare comfort as the morning offered and squeezed fleeting pleasure from such moments, no matter how short the duration. Within minutes after the monsoon-like rain ceased, at first light, the ever-present, bloodsucking mosquitoes would saturate every cubic foot of atmosphere near ground level, turning the moisture laden atmosphere into a kind of living, noncombatant hell.

Now and then I would silently admonish myself for allowing a thoughtless, dangerous impulse to dart through my mind: *Perhaps I should fly an extra mission so I could escape the villainous vermin in the cool, air-conditioned cockpit.* Then rational thought returned: Mosquitoes never shot down pilots; missiles and shrapnel sometimes did!

My last scheduled reconnaissance mission of the day would take my crew and me north in the Gulf of Tonkin west of Hainan Island, China. We were scheduled to reconnoiter enemy electronic emissions out of Hanoi and south to Vinh. Our track would take us parallel to the west coast of Hainan

Island into the sensitive northern reaches of Tonkin Gulf.

I oversaw my navigator's work with intense interest. I had great faith in Lt. Kevin Mason's proficiency and good common sense.

Kevin, a thin, six foot, well-tanned athlete who kept in prime shape by swimming and jogging whenever he found enough time, was a close friend at the time. He was a proficient navigator and therefore was not the least offended by my close supervision. Early on, we had made a pact that whenever we flew together, we always had license to respectfully double check each other's logic, procedures and work, particularly on hazardous missions. I trusted his excellent emotional control and abundance of good common sense he brought to his combat air crewmanship.

He and I had earlier discussed what consequences would likely result if our flight path should stray eastward to China's Hainan Island or too far north of Hanoi toward mainland China. We knew the Chi Com Air Force would be on us and would not hesitate to shoot us down. There would be no regrets.

Fortunately, most of our flight was scheduled to be more westerly toward the Vietnamese coast. We took great care to remain out of range of known North Vietnamese SAM (surface to air missile) sites. Most of the mission called for excellent navigation, vigilant data collection, and a healthy concern for potential air traffic out of Hainan Island and mainland China.

Our mission was routine and near completion when we received word that the Viet Cong had commenced rocket and mortar attacks on DaNang Air Base. We were directed to divert to Korat Air Base in northern Thailand until notified that the attacks on "home plate" (our home airfield) had terminated.

Lt. Mason, with professional anticipation, was prepared for that contingency and quickly supplied me with magnetic heading, range, and estimated time of arrival at Korat. I responded with an in-flight check and "fuel remaining" report. The aircrew stowed all loose gear.

I climbed to a higher altitude to avoid as much antiaircraft flak as possible and flew a circuitous route across North Vietnam to avoid known SAM sites en route.

At best, route changes to avoid SAM sites were a dangerous guessing game since the enemy frequently changed the locations of their SAM launchers and fire control equipment, setting up possible lethal consequences. The SAM launchers were on rubber tires and could easily be moved anywhere.

Approaching Korat Air Base, I called Korat Control Tower for clearance and landing instructions. All went smoothly, and soon we had landed and were taxiing to our designated parking area. We finished refueling our bird and were pleased and relieved to have a few hours rest and some food before we would fly back into Vietnam, the war, and recovery at DaNang. By then the hit and flee Viet Cong would have completed their rocket and mortar attacks on the military installations and would again have blended into the countryside.

The aircrew was not surprised when I released them to their own recognizance until midnight, DaNang time, so they could eat and rest—no alcohol before flying and drugs were never allowed! My policy was well known among my flight crew members. Violators would kiss their flight pay and flying goodbye forever if they made such a grievous error and I learned of it. Acts such as that could jeopardize the safety and lives of others in the crew. Zero tolerance was the only acceptable doctrine to assure our mutual survivability.

My briefing also disallowed departure from the air base proper or fraternizing with Thai civilian personnel. No discussion of flight schedules or missions was to be conducted with anyone who had no "need to know." We would rendezvous at 2400 hours (midnight) at our aircraft on the flight line.

I treated Lt. Mason to a meal in the Korat Officers Club at the "dirty shirt mess" where officers in flight suits on duty were excused from uniform regulations, this because of the close vicinity of a hot war just a flight hour to the east. During our meal, we overheard conversations about an unknown number of Thai Coms (Communist militants) who had earlier infiltrated Korat Air Base disguised as monks dressed in saffron colored religious robes.

Clever! One could hide all kinds of small arms, grenades, and weapons under those robes.

We departed for the flight line and our aircraft an hour before our scheduled rendezvous. The aircrew members had also heard about the Thai-Com infiltration. Sporadic small arms fire could be heard from the flight line.

I ordered the crew to prepare our bird for "start engines and flight," and to remain with the aircraft and stay alert while I was briefed in the operations hanger on the Thai Com situation. I arranged for a swift clearance for takeoff once I started engines and taxied to the runway.

The Thai Operations Duty Officer spoke reasonably good English—certainly much better than my Thai!

He informed me that "more than ten" Thai Coms had been killed and that some had been captured.

I knew I must get airborne as soon as possible. The irony of diverting from recovery at DaNang to a probable shooting gallery at Korat did not amuse me at all! The duty officer assured me that he would inform control tower personnel that I wanted expeditious takeoff clearance once I started engines.

I sprinted back to the aircraft.

Lt. Mason had completed the pre start check list in my absence. This was typical of Kevin as an outstanding navigator. He thought ahead and anticipated!

"Good thinking!" I commented as I signaled for "start engines" Anything to get out of there fast!

We taxied to the take off end of the runway. I turned off my exterior aircraft lights to make any sniper's efforts more difficult. As we approached the end of the taxi way, I radioed tower for immediate takeoff as planned.

To my annoyance, chagrin, and frustration, I was ordered to stop taxiing immediately!

Before I could challenge the control tower order, a helicopter flew very low over our aircraft and hovered momentarily over the end of the duty runway.

Suddenly, it climbed straight up to more than 100 feet above the runway and turned on a spotlight. As it hovered there, we could see a saffron-robed object dropping toward the concrete runway.

As it splattered at impact, we saw clearly that it had been a human.

A small arms tracer ricocheted past our cockpit. I immediately added a burst of thrust to my port engine and turned away from the source of the tracer. If we were going to take small arms fire, I wanted as much aircraft as possible between my crew and the incoming rounds.

No sooner than I had turned our aircraft empennage (tail) toward the unfriendly gunfire, a second saffron clad body hurtled from the helicopter to splat on the runway below. This time we saw that his ankles were bound together and his wrists tethered behind his back.

The helo was also under fire. Red tracers zipped past the helo as the pilot hung into position over the runway threshold.

We could see a third saffron robe in the helo doorway. He was not thrown out.

Quickly, an airfield truck arrived. Two men jumped out of the vehicle and pitched the grotesque, broken remains into the open truck box, and just as quickly, the truck sped swiftly away toward the Ops Building with its red grimes light flashing as it disappeared into the darkness.

The tower operator called our aircraft and cleared us for immediate take off while the speeding truck was still clearing the runway.

I did not hesitate. As our aircraft headed toward the runway centerline, I added full power, and we disappeared down the runway. I illuminated my exterior lights as the landing gear wheels lifted off the runway en route to DaNang.

We climbed rapidly for high altitude and chose as direct a route to DaNang as possible to keep us in country and away from known SAM sites so we would encounter less concentrated antiaircraft activity.

I informed my crew that Lt. Mason and I would debrief with the Intelligence personnel at DaNang after we landed. I asked that the men not tell exaggerated air stories about our adventures at Korat. The truth would eventually surface. In the meantime, I asked that we all concentrate on our own mission and stay alive.

The return flight to DaNang was performed in almost total silence as each of us silently relived that terror-filled scene. We were in varied states of shock, mesmerized by the incredulity of the sudden, unexpected drama that had played out before our eyes.

The whining turbojet engines; the whirring of the helo's rotor blades; the pitch blackness distorted by blue taxi way lights, green runway threshold lights, and the dim red cockpit instrument lights; the harsh glare of the helicopter floodlight; the sporadic small arms gunfire punctuated by muffled grenade concussions; the saffron robes floating almost languidly in a slow motion descent; the impact of flesh on concrete—our senses jangled with the unreality of those gut-wrenching moments. Man's inhumanity to man was never more clearly defined and demonstrated to my combat-seasoned crew. The surreal moments were as an irrational, incongruous nightmare that could never be erased from the memories of all of us who witnessed the event. As much as I had seen of death, I was not ready for that.

I was informed later at a 1st Marine Intelligence debriefing that what we had witnessed was probably a "routine" prisoner interrogation. If that was the case, I will wager all that I own that the third Thai Com prisoner who was next in line out of the helicopter door has not stopped volunteering answers to questions asked to this very day!

The way it was—Autumn, 1967.

CHAPTER 24—

SEABRINE AND THE RUSSIANS: OCTOBER, 1967

Another old, black limousine, almost like ours, approached.
As both cars slowed, we could see
that around the neck of each Russian hung a camera!
They were on the way to spy on us!

My combat crew and I had been back from a tour of duty out of DaNang Air Base, South Vietnam with VQ-1 for approximately one precious month, time when we had reconnected with our wives and children, had relaxed and lived, or pretended to live, like normal families, shopping, doing household repairs, going out to movies and dinner, visiting with friends. A month was a long time in our world, and we treasured every moment.

Then I received a "heads up" that I should prepare for a different venue in an extended deployment for Operation "Seabrine."

Operation Seabrine was a classified, highly secretive effort in the 1960's which involved tracking and shadowing Russian support group ships involved in ocean recovery of Russian reentry vehicles returning from outer space. When the Russians sent out their ships to a remote part of our area, we were there in the sky above them, tracking their movements, observing the splash down, photographing and electronically recording every part of their vehicle's return from space.

Our families had no notion of our tasks when we left home. We were simply gone and then we were back. What we had done was never discussed.

When I was assigned to Seabrine, I wore a different cap than when with VQ-1. I flew a prototype aircraft that was embedded in a squadron of similar looking aircraft at NAS Atsugi, Japan.

To the casual observer, the EA3B aircraft looked like the others, but the antennae were different, and inside the electronic devices were set for communication on the return of vehicles from outer space.

Even inside, it looked the same: four seats facing the port side of the aircraft in front of four consoles. The difference was that the consoles were manned not by Navy technicians but by Army Intelligence specialists under the command of Major Craig Loe

DEPARTMENT OF THE ARMY

THIS IS TO CERTIFY THAT
THE SECRETARY OF THE ARMY HAS AWARDED

THE ARMY COMMENDATION MEDAL

TO

LIEUTENANT COMMANDER ROBERT S. BEAT, UNITED STATES NAVY

FOR

MERITORIOUS SERVICE

JUNE 1967 TO APRIL 1968

GIVEN UNDER MY HAND IN THE CITY OF WASHINGTON
THIS   29th   DAY OF   OCTOBER   1969

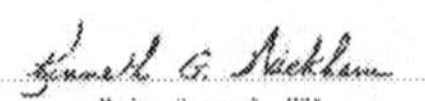

Very few Navy pilots have an Army Commendation Medal like this one. Mine came as a result of my piloting for Seabrine, the project that tracked Russian reentry vehicles from outer space. This was a combined effort by the National Security Agency (NSA) and the Army Security Agency (ASA). The U. S. Navy provided the air crew and prototype aircraft.

Seabrine was a highly classified operation that utilized this unusual combination: a Navy flight crew who were familiar with the flying terrain and ASA (Army Security Agency) personnel who were specially trained to operate the sophisticated electronic receivers located in a pressurized living compartment aft of the aircraft cockpit. The overall operation and data collection was under control of the National Security Agency.

The ASA specialists were tops in their lines of expertise. SFC Durwood "Woody" Black was the Flight Crew Technical System/Mission Coordinator. Acting Sergeant Ronald R. Shaw was the Team Chief. Specialist 5 James Pierce, Jr., a strapping Electronic System Operator later became a Warrant Officer. Mathew A. Nelson was an excellent Electronic Systems Operator, Frank Lovell, Jr. handled the ground equipment maintenance and repair as well as being an alternate on the Flight Crew.

I am certain that those who flew along on this particular Seabrine deployment will never forget the adventure.

After having participated in so many varied operations of very highly classified sensitivity, I could feel it, sense it, almost taste it—this trip would be special—one that should be interesting and memorable!

Every one in our seven man Seabrine crew had his own clearly spelled out responsibilities to attend to. They would complete their preparatory tasks and 24 hours prior to the deployment report to me as their pilot and Seabrine Commander. They would have been informed that the deployment was scheduled for that day, but they knew not to question where and why.

Dawn broke reluctantly on our scheduled special day. There was a broken 5000 foot layer of dreary gray clouds over Tokyo Bay. The sun showed promise of breaking through the clouds and appeared ready to send our crew and aircraft off on our deployment in great shape.

The crew had picked up my excitement…or perhaps they had heard rumors that this was a special flight that would take us to areas we had never overflown. For whatever reason, as we manned our bird, the excitement within the crew was obvious. All hands in the crew would be informed of our destination when there was no possibility of an inadvertent security leak.

Most of the crew's dependents were present to see their loved ones off though they did not know to what destination, only that this was to be a fairly long deployment. When crews depart, wives and children flock to see them off, with tearful heart-wrenching goodbyes and chins-up reassurances.

I always made my departure from Jan and our daughter privately in the parking area ahead of time.

The control tower was concise and prompt. My last second visual check of engine instruments all indicated, "Go!" My navigator, Dave Mercer, said, Off the deck exactly on time."

My Seabrine aircraft captain/flight engineer was busy checking all circuit breakers, buttoning up access hatches, double checking all switches and power sources for normal operation. Petty Officer John Purser had more experience at his Seabrine airborne duties than any other air crewman, performing all his responsibilities reliably and proficiently. As pilot and Seabrine Commander, I was pleased with my very proficient aircrew. Such performance always made flying safer and more enjoyable.

I turned my heavily loaded aircraft southward toward the North Philippines on a heading of south by southwest as I continued to expedite my climb to conserve fuel. All post take off check lists were quickly completed. Nothing left to chance—nothing forgotten. It was pure joy to fly with such great professionals, like Mercer and the Army Security Agency personnel.

Our flight plan for our first day was simple enough. Fly from NAS Atsugi, Japan to DaNang Air Base in South Vietnam, deliver mail for the VQ-1 officers and men stationed temporarily on that hellish cauldron of incessant nocturnal rocket and mortar attacks together with the blood sucking mosquito hoards. Also, we would deliver any needed aircraft parts to keep the DaNang aircraft in flying condition for combat support flights flown around the clock against the North Vietnam Forces north of the Demilitarized Zone (DMZ)

During our stop at DaNang, while my Seabrine crew was busy refueling our aircraft, I delivered classified mail to the Detachment Officer-in-Charge. None of us wished to remain in DaNang any longer than necessary.

We were airborne again in record time as we climbed to altitude while en route across Laos, Cambodia and Thailand for our overnight stop in Bangkok, Thailand. I cautioned my crew to return from liberty early, as I scheduled us to launch at first light the next morning.

They were beginning to raise questioning eyebrows that said, "and where might we be going?"

However, only Navigator Mercer and Major Loe and I knew our destination, this to assure that no slip-ups might compromise our mission. My air crew assumed I would tell them soon after we departed Bangkok and our "wheels were in the well" en route to our secret destination.

Seabrine 9, our aircraft, was at full throttle and racing down the Bangkok runway as the first ray of sunlight peeked at us from out to of the Cambodian jungle to our East. It immediately became clear to the crew that we were heading out over open waters, and post takeoff check lists were completed thoroughly in anticipation of a long flight with very few, if any,

friendly runways along our charted course in the event of an emergency .
After takeoff, I set the throttles at full thrust to climb to high altitude and
conserve fuel—always smart planning for the unexpected.

We continued our ascent to above flight level three two zero (32,000
ft.). While climbing, I adjusted our heading to the south-southwest so our
course would take us just south of Sri Lanka to avoid violating Sri Lankan
air space. Seabrine 9 passed east and well south of the southern tip of India
(Cape Comorin).

By this time my Seabrine air crew were almost beside themselves
with curiosity as to our mission and destination.

"OK, Commander, want to tell us where we're going?"

My answer? "Generally south."

At this point, I could have told them where we were going and why,
but instead, I had my navigator, Dave Mercer, announce on the aircraft
intercom that we would land and refuel on the island of Gan—a few meager miles south of the equator.

Gan Island was a good base to know about that deep in the Indian
Ocean where refueling bases were at a premium. It had an excellent British
jet airfield with attendant support. Gan is the most southern island of any
significance in the Maldive Island chain that extends all the way from India
to the Equator in the Indian Ocean and east of the African continent.

On Gan we learned that the native population was suffering from hundreds of cases of typhus and typhoid fever in epidemic numbers, and the
crew refueled in record time to get us out of there post haste.

When we were airborne, I finally relented! I told Major Loe to relieve
the tension and tell them.

"In a matter of less than three more hours of flight, we will land at our
operational destination at 20 degrees South Latitude, 57 degrees 30 East
Longitude on the then British protectorate of Mauritius Island."

They understood the significance of the journey. They were pioneers!
They were the very first squadron crew to penetrate so deeply into the
Indian Ocean. Being "First There" in VQ-1 or Seabrine was a rarity,
because the squadron personnel over many years had traveled far and wide
in performance of their military duties. Further, we could now tell them,
"We're here to spy on the Russians who have clustered ships in apparent
anticipation of a space reentry vehicle landing."

This was exciting stuff.

I think they instantly forgave me for holding out on them. One of the men came up behind me and expressed the thoughts of all the men: "Finally!" he said.

After our landing on the only jet runway at the south end of Mauritius, I communicated with a British Security Group stationed on Mauritius and set up a meeting to familiarize and coordinate communications and operational intentions.

DAY 2

Our initial meeting was at 1000 hours local time on the tarmac where Seabrine 9 was tied down. The British hosts had been good enough to arrange for a four door "limousine'" for our "official use" as the British Officer in Charge diplomatically put it, as he gave me the ignition key for the vehicle.

Our trusty charger was a limousine in name only. It was a battered, had-seen-better days, four door Ford of questionable vintage that rattled like a defective washing machine and had long since lost any semblance of springs as it jolted us across the tarmac.

We had no reason to complain since it was a real aid for our crew, better than hiking.

Our lodging was in a relatively nice resort beach hotel, the Le Chaland, about a mile and a quarter from the airfield.

The crew spent their working day preparing our aircraft for operational readiness and anticipated flight for familiarization purposes.

Navigator Dave Mercer and I studied some navigational charts provided to us by the British Security Group, charts that had excellent detail of the local area.

I drove with Mercer and Major Loe to the British Security Group location and there we were thoroughly briefed on what the British knew concerning the Russian support ships that were arriving at Port Louis Seaport on the northwest coast of Mauritius approximately 25 miles from the jet airport where our aircraft was located.

DAY 3

Seabrine 9 launched at 0600 local time to reconnoiter local islands and possible emergency landing sites, if any.

I remained totally clear of Port Louis. I did not want to alert the Russian support ship crews of my presence. They would know soon enough if a Russian reentry vehicle arrived from outer space.

I felt certain that the Russians were probably aware that an American Navy reconnaissance aircraft was already positioned on Mauritius, but we would give them no extra help.

By the time we had become acquainted with nearby islands and the paucity of alternate runways and/or emergency landing sites, I returned to land at Mauritius.

I don't know where the idea came from. Perhaps I had caught the excitement of the crew at the prospect of being full blown spies on the Russians. But there it was, full blown and irresistible!

"How many of you have cameras…and film?"
This one had a Leika. That one a long distance attachment, this a wide angled lens; every conceivable type and model as would be expected from technical men like this crew.

"We're going to man the stealth operation of the century! I announced. "Port Louis here we come! "
They caught on at once. We were going to do the James Bond thing!
We piled into our old limousine and proceeded toward Port Louis on the best—and only—road on our impromptu spying photo recon mission.
We planned to surreptitiously make our clandestine move from ashore in the harbor and take many photos of the Russian ships' superstructures and every antenna array on all the ships. By the placement and direction of the antennae, we could hopefully read the Russians' intentions.
Everything proceeded like clockwork. I drove with Loe in front, and Mercer and the other three in back. I had left one Army man to guard our aircraft.
It was a lark. "Those super-dumb Russkies! We, the incredible spies! We'll whip their butts!"

There was almost no traffic, and we were almost halfway there when we saw a car approaching, another old, black limousine, almost like ours. This one was also packed with heads. But the heads were adorned with the red and gold insignia of the Soviet Union.
Both cars slowed as we passed each other. We could see that around the neck of each Russian hung a camera!

They were on the way to spy on us!

The occupants of both limos burst out laughing and we all gave each other the Navy one fingered salute as a semi-friendly gesture. The scene had degenerated into a Looney Tunes cartoon comedy.

A short distance ahead, I spotted a roadside shop that had a telephone. We hurriedly stopped and I called the British Security Group to tell them what was happening. When they finally stopped laughing, I requested that they notify the security guard I had assigned to our aircraft to lock our aircraft and cover all appropriate antennae from curious Russian cameras—all was not lost.

I did have a gnawing feeling in my gut that perhaps the Russians might have had radio contact between their limo and their ships. Since I could not control that; we would continue doggedly to complete our glorious spying mission.

Russian fighters like this one, sometimes were vectored out over the Sea of Japan to check on VQ-1 reconnaissance aircraft. Fortunately, they made passes without using their ordnance.

The roadside market was an interesting bit of local merchandising. We hurriedly perused their wares, some familiar, some exotic: potatoes, carrots, sugar cane, rice, bamboo, corn, tropical fruits, clothing and local textiles, several pastries—mostly cookies. I recognized none. Tea and coffee. There was a fine display of fish, calamari, crabs, and something I would describe as seaweed.

I had had a good meal of locally caught fish the previous evening and was happy to discover that same fish for sale in the market, a "snook fish", a mean looking, percoid sports fish slightly resembling a Northern Pike found in fresh water lakes and streams in the Great Lakes states back home. The snook attains a length of nearly a meter and a half when mature and tastes good when properly prepared.

I'm happy, however, to have tasted it after it had been dressed and broiled—not when I first saw it pulled out of the Indian Ocean!

Tempus fugit!

I collected my cheerful, joking camera crew and we continued toward our photo targets in Port Louis, the capital city of Mauritius, where we had a heyday photographing Russian ships and their antennae arrays by the dozens, far more revealing and significant than anything the Russians could have shot.

We stopped and dropped off our films with the British and requested their assistance processing our photographic "booty," offering them *carte blanche* on any copies they wished to duplicate. I knew they would copy them anyway, but I wanted them to know I appreciated their assistance and we wished to cooperate wherever we could.

The British were still chuckling about our Russian encounter when we departed to return to our Seabrine 9 aircraft.

The Security Group personnel laughed that our trip to Port Louis was more excitement and hilarity that they had enjoyed in months. Mauritius was a far piece from the beaten track. British dry humor is priceless and we thoroughly enjoyed working with them.

I wonder if the British have stopped laughing yet about the Russian and American spies.

I know that my crew still chuckles when they reminisce about the "Port Louis photo coup d'etat"

Seabrine 9 was locked; all sensitive antennae were covered; the Russians could have obtained no pictures of significance.

In the last analysis, the American photo team got their photos. The Russians did not! The "good guys" won in a close photo finish!

DAY 4

However, Robert Burns said it best. "The best laid plans of .mice and men aft gang agley."

Some time shortly before noon local time, the British Security Group received a coded message and delivered same to me. The message was terse and without explanation.

"Return at once to home base via the same route and stops performed during your deployment.

No reason why. Just return.

Our only response possible was a "Yes, Sir!"

Our spying days were over before they had really begun!

I called an immediate meeting at the aircraft and sent our limo to retrieve two crewmen who had checked out to go to the Le Chaland Hotel. I had previously cautioned the crew that nothing was to be mentioned to anyone as to any departure routes and/or destinations.

In the meeting, we decided to interpret the "at once" message. Major Loe and Lt. Mercer concurred that departing early morning on Day 5 was more prudent than leaving late evening on Day 4. None of us wished to risk any unpredictable delays at Gan Island which might delay us overnight, considering the serious epidemic problem there with typhus and typhoid.

Then, there could be the ensuing possibility of late departure from Gan which could exacerbate an extremely long flying day further, arriving at Bangkok, Thailand, exhausted, sleep deprived and mal nourished. We then would still have a long day of substantial flight time remaining before arriving at "home plate—NAS Atsugi, Japan."

O530 Day 5

The Gods of Flight were with us on this day. We were airborne out of Mauritius at 0630 local time and climbed to FL 290 (29,000 ft.) enroute to Gan Island. Everything happened on schedule and we had no problems to Gan Island nor to Bangkok where we arrived late afternoon.

A very ironic happenstance was in the making on this day in Bangkok. Unbeknown to my wife, Jan, and to me, both of us were in Bangkok simultaneously. While I was deployed to some "unknown location" on earth for some "unknown length of time," Jan and the Commanding Officer's wife decided to take a shopping tour of the Orient. As the gods of fate would have it, the shoppers arrived in Bangkok a couple of hours before my arrival there from the Equator out of the Indian Ocean! Neither of us knew the other was there, nor did we discover what could have been a joyous surprise reunion until several days later in Japan. C'est la vie!

0600 Day 6

All hands were up and seemed fairly well rested. Major Loe had arranged for a "gee dunk" truck with soft drinks and sandwiches to arrive at the flight area which really was a blessing. The aircrew ate reasonably well. Following food, we all got down to serious business. The aircraft was up and ready.

No one complained about departing Bangkok for the long journey to home base. I think everyone was anxious to be back with loved ones, grateful that their expected long, adventurous expedition had become a short, humorous one.

Bright and early, the morning sun peeked through the same Cambodian jungle at Seabrine 9. I made a sharp turn to port while climbing for altitude to discourage any gooks from attempting small arms target practice at our aircraft. I remained on a course south of the DMZ as I entered Laotian airspace heading east for my descent over the Gulf of Tonkin. DaNang Tower gave me landing clearance and the rest was easy. I contacted the O inC (Officer in Charge) of the VQ-1 Detachment and requested any mail and/or parts for transport to home plate.

It was approximately 0900 when we manned our aircraft for takeoff. It was very humid and the temperature on the parking ramp had already exceeded 90 degrees F. We closed all hatches and I turned on the pressurization and air conditioning: My aircrew cheered in happy relief.

Seabrine 9 and aircrew were commencing the last leg of our homeward bound journey. It was a significant distance but it always seemed much longer than usual because of the crew's anxiety to be back with their dependents and friends.

I suspect many of them broke secrecy vows to share their "spy" adventure.

We still had to circumnavigate China while remaining over the South China Sea clear of Chinese airspace. Lastly, I would fly a beeline from the south end of Taiwan past Okinawa, then south of Kyushu, Shikoku, and the western half of Honshu, Japan. Seabrine 9 and aircrew landed safely at NAS Atsugi, Japan. We arrived mid afternoon on Day 6 to joyful tears and happy reunions.

The "long" deployment had lasted less than a week!

We were never debriefed on what purpose we were intended to perform. I did not ask: I had had many missions previously and knew the usual answer from NSA.

"You have no need to know."

It took practice, patience, and some blind loyalty to accept such an inadequate explanation. This fire drill had enough clues to be at least semi-transparent. We had tracked the Russian support ships general departure movement since they were good enough to depart from Port Louis Harbor on Mauritius Island during the darkness of night. Their general movement did not provide much concealment in the Indian Ocean where Seabrine 9 could overtake them at closing speeds of up to 600 to 700 miles an hour faster than they could run away.

Apparently the space craft had not landed near there after all. Perhaps it was never planned to land there.

The sum of accrued knowledge through experience with NSA allowed our crew to sometimes divine more knowledge than NSA gave us credit for. No further inquiries were made and none were needed. Through repetition, exposure, and operational participation, an individual could become very knowledgeable if one survived long enough.

It was good to be home in Japan.

CHAPTER 25—

THE PUEBLO—DECEMBER 1967

*I was struck by how gray Commander Bucher looked—
pale, almost—quite unlike the usual ruddy, tanned coloration of a
skipper.
His face was deeply grooved and lined.
His forehead was carved deeply with wrinkles indicating worry and
strain.*

I've always been inquisitive by nature, but never more so than when the object of my curiosity had direct bearing on my personal safety. It was not unusual to discover that maintaining that healthy curiosity about my military environment occasionally offered rewarding outcomes.

Because of my natural compulsion to investigate whatever I felt could change my Electronic Intelligence reconnaissance environment or personal survival odds, I was, for part of one day, aboard the doomed USS Pueblo. I met and talked with Commander Lloyd Bucher, Commanding officer of the Pueblo, for a brief period while aboard his ship on Navy business.

The Pueblo was destined for disastrous misfortune in the Sea of Japan less than one month after my conversation with Commander Bucher, but neither of us was aware of this during our discussion on a frigid winter day in December, 1967.

This was not a chance meeting but one that I arranged.

The Pueblo was classified as an AGER ship, one that was supposed to be collecting information about the environment—soundings, etc., but with my clearance, I knew that while the Pueblo was docked, that some highly sensitive classified electronic equipment was due to be installed in the Pueblo. This completely belied the stated purpose of the ship and clued me in that this was a ship that would be part of the spying runs that I would be flying over the Sea of Japan

I had read and heard highly sensitive message traffic that suggested the role of the Pueblo in the spying missions under way.

I needed to know more about it.

My squadron, VQ-1, had grown and mushroomed into the largest U. S. Navy aviation squadron in modern times during the early 1960's. This was primarily caused by the ever-increasing need for electronic intelligence (ELINT) in the Western Pacific and Southeast Asia theaters. VQ-1 was over-tasked supporting the war effort in Vietnam.

The squadron detachment at DaNang Air Base just south of the Demilitarized Zone (DMZ) had at least one VQ-1 aircraft airborne over the North Vietnam sector 24 hours every day of the year from 1965 through the end of hostilities in 1969.

Additionally, the squadron surveilled the Chinese coast throughout the South China Sea and into the Sea of Japan. This also included the large island of Hainan in the Gulf of Tonkin.

Furthermore, the coast lines of North Korea and Russia on the western and northern shores, respectively of the Sea of Japan were "garden spots" under surveillance by VQ-1. All those vast areas required varying portions of the VQ-1's 1,000 officers and sailors' ELINT surveillance efforts.

It was a momentous, overwhelming, long-term task.

I finished briefing my relief as officer-in-charge of the VQ-1 Detachment, DaNang, by 1100 hours. My crew and I were airborne for Atsugi, Japan at high noon...to wives and families...or lady friends.

I piloted my aircraft and crew nonstop from DaNang across the South China Sea, remaining well clear of the Chinese coat to avoid any conflict with the Chinese Air Defenses. I then turned northeastward, passing just south of Taiwan and the East China Sea.

My crew was always anxious when we passed the southern tip of Taiwan.

We had a little game we played. As pilot, in a loud, officious voice, I would transmit on the aircraft intercom: "Navigator, set the beeline!"

All hands shouted, yelled and applauded. They knew I was about to take one heading—straight as an arrow—that would take us directly to Atsugi. The changes in my beeline heading would be minor to compensate for changes in winds aloft, directions, and intensities. My beeline would be approximately 1,340 nautical miles long. It is seldom that a pilot flies a beeline that far in the Orient.

We all had loved ones excitedly waiting to see that homeward bound aircraft arrive!

I was attached to Fleet Air Reconnaissance Squadron One (VQ-1) during that year as an Electronic Warfare Aircraft Commander. VQ-1 was based at U. S. Naval Air Station, Atsugi, Japan—less than a one hour drive from the Japanese Seaport of Yokosuka on the edge of Tokyo Bay.

When we were back at home base in Atsugi and not on a flying assignment, I resumed my squadron assignment as an officer in the Maintenance Department.

This time, I immediately made arrangements to get myself assigned to the delivery of supersensitive equipment to the Pueblo. Again, I simply needed to know what was happening in the electronic spying game.

The Japanese rainy season (nubei) had come and gone, but the weather that December was cold with more than enough monsoon rains. The Japanese islands were annually threatened by typhoons generated and fueled by warm, tropical sea waters between the equator and 2 N latitude. Such cyclonical storms originated south of the Philippine Islands and as far west as Sumatra.

Fortunately, this year, Japan had been spared the most severe winds and flooding damage during the late summer and fall months. The weather, however, was unusually overcast that winter of 1967. Arctic gusty winds penetrated every part of Yokosuka Harbor and turned noses red and fingers inside cold weather gloves stiff and numb.

On the designated date at the appointed hour, five "spooks" (electronic technicians with compartmented security clearance) and I loaded tool boxes and special equipment into our assigned battered gray Navy carryall.

All of us in heavy, foul-weather winter gear crowded into the overloaded vehicle. The driver turned on the heater to defrost the coated windshield, and in moments, we were all steamingly hot. I quickly put an end to the farce by ordering everyone out except the driver until he could get windows and windshield cleared.

Seven or eight minutes later, we climbed back aboard, laughing, wisecracking, blaming the driver for not procuring a better vehicle from the motor pool. We bumped and lurched our way as the driver tried to avoid some very nasty, deep, water-filled potholes on the winter damaged roads that led to Yokosuka Harbor.

We arrived at Yokosuka at 0800—38 minutes en route, exactly on schedule.

Our driver was familiar with the warehouse area where the classified equipment had been pre-positioned in a drab looking, small warehouse under heavily armed guard. I was relieved that our driver located the warehouse quickly since all building signs had lots of Kanji—Japanese characters—with very few English letters or Arabic numerals.

This was a Japanese stratagem to keep uncleared personnel from discovering the central, highly sensitive, classified storage location where large quantities of compartmented materials were secreted under intense security at all times.

I scanned the area and quickly surmised that the permanent storage area was probably in one of the maze of tunnels that had been blasted from the solid rock hills and accessed only through heavily timbered, giant doors—all of which were securely locked. These tunnel storage areas were constructed during W.W.II to keep enemy aircraft from bombing and destroying explosive munitions, flammable materials, etc.

I stayed in the vehicle while two of the men went in and came out with two innocuous looking crates. They could have picked up bananas, or beer, or toilet paper. After I receipted for the boxes of materials, we proceeded to the Pueblo which was not far away—perhaps one or two miles at most in the harbor docking area.

We parked the vehicle close to the ship's gangway so we did not have extra difficulty getting the special equipment on the ship.

The USS Pueblo was an unimposing vessel. Any observers who may have noticed the 170 1/2 foot ship arrive probably assumed the Pueblo was in port for provisions, minor repairs, and upkeep. It had a 10 foot draft, a beam width of 221' 8". The power plant was two-diesel engines and two propellers with a maximum (flank) speed of 12.6 knots.

Even its history was unimpressive. The diminutive ship was built and launched from a shipyard in Kewaunee, Wisconsin on 16 April 1944, during WW II. Ten years later the auxiliary vessel was mothballed in 1954. Later, in April 1966 the little, antiquated ship was retrofitted and transferred to the U. S. Navy, renamed the USS Pueblo. The vessel still lacked watertight integrity and required additional updating of equipment.

I didn't know it at the time, and have only learned about the real lack of equipment by reading some of the many books that have been written about the illegal boarding and the vile mistreatment of the Commander and his men.

This supposed "environmental research" ship had been assigned by the officer in charge at CINCPACFLT to the Sea of Japan in close proximity to Wonsan, North Korea, a risk assessment of "minimal," and Commander Bucher had repeatedly and unsuccessfully tried to get the assessment upgraded to 'hazardous."

While in Yokosuka, he also requested updated, more efficacious equipment for destruction of highly sensitive codes, classified publications and ELINT receivers. Such equipment was to be utilized to destroy codes, publications, cipher equipment and ELINT receivers if capture was imminent, and/or sinking of the Pueblo was probable. Again, his request had been denied.

It was unlikely that there were any armed boats or ships in the North Korean Navy that were as poorly and inadequately armed as the USS Pueblo. The only ship armament aboard the USS Pueblo were two W.W.II type 50 caliber machine guns. One of the guns was reported as malfunctioning before the ship's arrival in Yokosuka, but no in-port repairs were performed on the guns. Inadequate, if any, armor plating was installed around the machine gun mounts on the open weather deck of the Pueblo. The gun crews of the two 50 caliber guns without protection of armor would be completely vulnerable and exposed to hostile fire.

The ship was a sitting duck!

All I knew, when we approached the ship, was that it was a small, tired looking vessel that would soon have equipment far too sophisticated to be used for "environmental research."

The Pueblo was simply a spy ship.

On the dock below the ship, two sailors with side arms were posted near ship cartons and supplies—nothing unusual to draw the suspicious attention. We had clearance, so when we climbed the ramp to board the ship, other men, also with side arms, saluted and let us through. A Pueblo work party arrived to assist my technicians in taking equipment inside the ship, unpacking it out of sight for security reasons.

As I scanned the bridge and the ships superstructure upon my arrival, it was obvious to me that the equipment update was needed. The obvious hydrographer's props displayed visibly on the weather deck of the Pueblo did not hoodwink nor deceive me because I had read the traffic messages and knew this was a spy ship as much as the aircraft I flew was an espionage vessel. The ship was intended to and may have appeared authentic to less informed observers.

I inquired of the officer of the deck at the gangway if Cdr. Bucher was aboard. I was informed he was on the bridge and would be at the gangway shortly. The Commanding Officer arrived soon thereafter.

Bucher double checked the bills of lading to verify that the correct materials and quantities had come aboard. When the Skipper finished the inventory, I stepped forward and snapped a sharp salute.

Bucher looked startled but returned my salute as I introduced myself. I gave him a copy of my crew's names and security clearances, including my own.

He was quite congenial and invited me to the bridge where we could have a more private conversation. He wasted no time getting down to business. I knew he was aware of the answers before he asked the questions. He was testing me to ascertain if I had knowledge about ELINT and generally about the use of the equipment we had delivered to the Pueblo. Bucher seemed pleasantly surprised that I could carry on an intelligent conversation about our ELINT roles in the Japanese Sea.

I was pleased that Commander Bucher did not try to "blow smoke" at me about hydrography. After all, he had just read my security clearance, and I earlier had delivered sensitive, compartmented ELINT receivers to him. As we spoke, my maintenance "spooks" were installing that state-of-the-art spy gear into his ship!

He, of course, had implied that the Pueblo was an ELINT collector and was under the direct control of the National Security Agency. When I asked about the ship, he smiled wryly and said that their role was far removed from the war, concerned with the field of hydrography. I played his game and asked about the tasks of the environmental research.

Cdr. Bucher nonchalantly said that his requests to improve the Pueblo's readiness had been "delayed." He also stated that the Pueblo was under direct control of the NSA, but this I already knew because of the previous message traffic to VQ-1.

No mention was made of the ship's actual mission or war plans. What he may have known still remains the subject of much speculation in the many books written on the situation.

I was struck by how gray he looked—pale, almost—quite unlike the usual ruddy, tanned coloration of a skipper. His face was deeply grooved and lined. His forehead was carved with wrinkles that indicated worry and strain.

All I could think of was a quotation I had once read, "Decision making is encumbered by the liability of consequences." Somehow I knew that this was to be Lloyd Bucher's fate as long as he was commanding officer of the USS. Pueblo. His inner self would compel him to remain unchanged as long as he carried out his role as Commanding Officer. He was not going to make waves though deep inside, he must have known that something was gravely wrong!

In the course of our conversation, I was tempted to mention to Cdr. Bucher that I had earlier been a pilot assigned to fly missions for NSA and the U. S. Army Security Agency (ASA) with Seabrine concerning Russian reentry vehicles returning from outer space but decided against the urge. Bucher seemed very preoccupied and likely not to give a damn. I avoided that issue and later was pleased that I did, since, as so often is the case with NSA business, he had "no need to know."

The VQ-1 "spooks" completed the installations and continuity checks. Cdr. Bucher and I waited for my technicians to pack up their tool boxes and equipment. When completed, they joined us on the quarterdeck for our departure to return to NAS Atsugi. Bucher returned my salute as I disembarked from the Pueblo. It was the first and last time I would ever see him.

The conversation in our vehicle was subdued and somewhat limited en route to Atsugi. Though I said nothing about our conversation, I mused quietly about what I had learned and what must have been passing through Cdr. Bucher's mind. I had no clue at that time. Could he have suspected that he might not have been completely or honestly briefed on the Pueblo's mission and/or war plan? That he was slated to become a pawn between the CIA and NSA, as others now affirm?

On Jan. 5, 1968 the Pueblo quietly slipped out of Yokosuka Harbor and went down to sea for passage to Sasebo, Japan. Pueblo and crew had a short turn around in Sasebo and went down to sea on Jan. 10, departing initially west by southwest, en route to the Sea of Japan. They eventually traversed the Korean Strait eastern channel between Honshu, Japan, and South Korea into the Sea of Japan. .

The USS Pueblo cruised slowly into the Japanese Sea while maintaining its ruse of being involved in environmental research in the field of hydrography. The ship progressed slowly northward west of Hiroshima, Japan. Days later when the North Koreans became aware of the Pueblo in the Sea of Japan, their surveillance and harassment efforts began and intensified as the Pueblo moved northwest toward Wonsan. By January 22, 1968 the harassment intensified and threats of boarding were numerous.

While all this was transpiring, I often visited in the underground, high security communications center with my eyes glued to the incoming Pueblo traffic reports. It was as though I had a front row seat at an action packed chess game of war, real time! Except this time I knew the ship and identified with the Skipper.

Midday on 23 January, the Chinese boarded and seized the Pueblo. The captors were unmistakably Chinese and were easily identified since they were wearing Chinese Army uniforms. The Pueblo crew resolutely continued to send SOS messages as the Chinese searched the ship.

This activity was abruptly stopped by a Russian destroyer that had appeared suddenly and took the USS Pueblo under fire. A Soviet cannon shell hit the ship and killed a U. S. sailor and seriously wounded several others. The Russians boarded the Pueblo and thoroughly searched the ship. After they ended their search, they released the Pueblo to the North Korean boarding party and returned to their destroyer.

The North Koreans "captured" the Pueblo at that moment. The Pueblo was commandeered by the North Koreans at 1432 local time on 23 January, 1968, and taken into the Wonsan Harbor as the equivalent of a war prize.

Those of us who were monitoring this epoch in the communications center hundreds of miles from the actual scene were stunned, in denial, and frustrated beyond measure.

Did this really happen?

How could the United States Navy and Air Force allow this upstart, barbaric country ruled by a madman to capture and steal a Navy warship on the international high seas without one modicum of resistance?

Ridiculous!! Unbelievable!!

All of us knew that there were hundreds of U. S. 5th Air Force and U. S. Navy fighters available to defend the ship. Our frustrations were intense because we knew there were actions that could be employed to change the tide of battle in favor of the Pueblo. My anger was more intense than most because I had been so recently with the commander on his ship.

Commander Lloyd Bucher suffered imprisonment, torture, and merciless beatings from North Korean guards. Upon release from North Korean imprisonment, he was returned to California to be pilloried in a farcical Navy court martial which convicted him of dereliction of duty. That edict was later reversed by the Secretary of the Navy.

Lloyd Bucher, Commander, U. S. Navy, Commanding Officer of the USS Pueblo (AGER-2) died about a year after his reinstatement, a broken and embittered man.

The final chapter of the Pueblo story may still be unwritten. The diminutive United States warship remains in Wonsan Harbor. It is still a commissioned ship in the U. S. Navy which resolutely continues in a geopolitical taffy pull with the government of North Korea as to the ownership of the Pueblo.

Some future day, I would like to revisit that historic ship and silently reminisce about all that happened in the Sea of Japan while I helplessly monitored the USS Pueblo message traffic in safety hundreds of miles away at NAS Atsugi, Japan.

CHAPTER 26—

THE DRAGON LADY— THE YEAR OF THE U-2

Never quite sure how or why I was selected,
I still felt that I was the chosen one
when I flew the fabulous U-2.

It was a cold Monday night in October 1974. I walked briskly from my parked auto to the meeting and banquet room near the Pacific Ocean surf in Ventura California. I was excited to attend this particular monthly gathering and dinner of the Oxnard-Santa Barbara Hangar of the Quiet Birdmen—an invitation only group of retired military and civilian pilots who are never quite willing to let go of their love of flying.

We invariably had interesting, highly experienced speakers invited to visit our monthly meetings and brief the Quiet Birdmen on scientific and aeronautical related developments.

The speaker of our October meeting was a good friend I had not seen for two or three years. I felt certain his speech would be stimulating and provide the Q.B. aviators with highly interesting aviation updates from the Lockheed Aircraft Corporation.

Our speaker on this particular evening was Ben Rich, the retired manager of the Lockheed Skunkworks. Prior to 1975 when Clarence "Kelly" Johnson retired, Rich had been Johnson's assistant manager and right hand man in the development of many highly classified aeronautical projects at Lockheed.

During the early 1950's, such incredible aircraft as the U-2 and the SR71 high-flying spy aircraft were invented by the Lockheed Skunkworks. Sophisticated aircraft, such as these, were planned, drafted, engineered and assembled years ahead of their time.

This was best expressed by a sign I read over the door where I entered the Skunkworks during my first visit. The sign read, "You are entering the

Lockheed Skunkworks. Set your watches ahead 20 years!"
In retrospect, I think it may have been true!

Ben Rich gave the Quiet Birdmen a wonderful speech filled with much heretofore undisclosed, recently declassified information and data about the high-flying U-2 and SR71 reconnaissance aircraft. He had the listeners in the meeting sitting of the front edges of their chairs, wholly absorbed in his every description and statement. He then invited questions from his rapt audience following his speech. There were dozens of well-thought out questions that Ben answered fully.

However, as the "Q and A" period continued, I began to feel uneasy. I could divine where these questions inevitably were leading. Soon thereafter, one of my Q.B. friends inquired of Ben Rich if he knew of any U-2 or SR71 pilots who were retired and living in Ventura County or nearby environs.

Ben paused, smiled, and collected his lecture notes. He looked up and said, "I do believe there is at least one U-2 pilot in this area." He was wearing a wide grin.

He pointed at me and said, "Scott Beat, stand up!"

Prior to that defining moment, I had not divulged that information to anyone—not even to my wife! No one, not even she, had a need to know.

I was always concerned with the paper-thin line between classified and unclassified information.

When I left the Navy, I was sworn to secrecy about where I had gone and the work I had done—what I had done during my years with VQ-1 and Seabrine, and most important, even the fact that I had been a U-2 pilot.

I had never had difficulty in keeping secrets. If you tell no one, then simply, the secret is not divulged! The National Security Agency taught me that many years before, and I have always been appalled by the number of people who seemingly cannot comprehend and conform to such a simple premise.

Among the numerous happenstances of my turbulent military years of serving my country as a naval aviator and aircraft carrier pilot, there were events that occurred by design and many that occurred by chance. Often, I would learn classified information which came and went and no action was taken. The "secrets" or events simply deteriorated into insignificance and were lost with the passage of time. Or I would meet one of the giants of the time and brush shoulders with history.

Such was the case of my chance meeting with Clarence "Kelly" Johnson when I was at Lockheed Corporation in Los Angeles, California on totally unrelated Navy business in 1956.

Johnson had been one of only a handful of aeronautical engineers on Lockheed's payroll in the early 1950's. His employers quickly recognized that this aero engineer was talented and had boundless energy. He often thought outside the psychological "box" that entraps and inhibits many engineers in the performance of their engineering duties and problem solving. In short order, Johnson was made overseer of the Lockheed Skunkworks.

This was/is a select special projects group that handled many compartmented, highly sensitive and classified aeronautical projects assigned to the Lockheed Corporation.

The day of my visit, it was my good fortune to be introduced to and become acquainted with "Kelly" Johnson. We bonded easily when we discovered a mutual, intense interest in aviation. I would have happily followed Kelly around just to have the privilege and opportunity to learn aero engineering and aircraft production from this great man. I knew, however, he was too over scheduled for that to ever happen.

Thereafter, whenever I had, or could manufacture a reason, I would make the trip back to the Skunkworks to learn and observe as much as possible. I didn't know it at the time I met Johnson, but I was to fly one of the aircraft he had just put in service.

President Dwight D. Eisenhower, during the USA-Soviet Union cold war, sensed an intense urgency from a Soviet Union covert nuclear weapons threat. To counter this, President Eisenhower organized, authorized, and expedited a highly classified group effort to develop an ultra high flying spy aircraft, one that hopefully could over fly the Soviet Union at altitudes so high that the Soviets would be unable to intercept and destroy the high-flying reconnaissance spy aircraft with either ground to air missiles or air to air missiles. It was a joint effort of the Central Intelligence Agency, the US Air Force, Lockheed Aircraft Corporation, and other defense contractors,

The President assigned that formidable task to Lockheed and Kelly Johnson was put in charge in 1952. CIA was to finance the project. Kelly once told me that Eisenhower had invited four men to share the responsibility for heading the project, but that he, Kelly, had refused to participate under those circumstances. "Too damn many cooks in the kitchen," he told the President, and Eisenhower gave him complete control.

The program was named Aquatone. Incredibly, the Aquatone Project produced and test flew the first Aquatone aircraft in August, 1955. Lockheed Head Test Pilot, Tony Leviere, was the first pilot to successfully fly the new spy aircraft.

Thus evolved the high altitude, top secret, covert reconnaissance missions over the Soviet Union utilizing U-2 spy aircraft in 1956. The missions were code-named "Operation Overflight" by President Eisenhower.

It was 1968. I was fatigued, dehydrated and had little, if any, feeling remaining in my gluteus muscles as I continued to descend for recovery at Bodo Airfield on the west coast of Norway near the Arctic Circle.

I was one with my Dragon Lady—my precious U-2—and yet I could hardly wait to get away from her. She was a sultry temptress who had asked too much of me, had drained my vitality.

The descent from very high altitude we had flown was relatively routine, quite unlike the flight itself. It was a welcome half hour when I could let my thoughts stray from the extreme concentration. I could flex my toes to stimulate my blood circulation and relax a bit to improve my mental acuity after more than a half dozen hours of enforced physical inactivity. It was good insurance for better keenness of perception during my forthcoming approach and landing at Bodo when the U-2 would again demand all my skill.

I was coaxing my Dragon Lady down from her lofty perch more that 70,000 feet above the earth. It took persistent patience and delicate airmanship to persuade my reluctant lady to descend from the heavens. She wanted to fly, not to land. She was built to soar and glide and tempt the stars, not sulk in an enclosed hanger.

The U-2 aircraft is not conventional when descending from ultra high altitudes.

As an experienced pilot, I would usually have pulled back the throttle, put out my speed brakes, and push my aircraft nose into a dive.

If I had done that to my Dragon Lady, she would have totally rebelled. As she cruised through the stratosphere at subsonic speeds, she needed consistency. An abrupt pull back of the throttle would slow her sharply and cause her to immediately decelerate below the safe air speed range.

Stall, flame out, and fall!

Death to the ship and the pilot!

She needed the sensuous, delicate touch. She would rather self destruct than be ordinary.

She is not, and was not intended to be, a stable training aircraft. She is a remarkable flying machine that can do some incredible things as long as I, as the pilot, know all of her performance characteristics and adhere rigidly to her very sensitive, special regime of flight.

I dance with her and she leads, but subtly so that I think I am in command.

She has her own unique requirements and will not tolerate deviations. She continually tests my flight experience, my expertise and airmanship, my aeronautical knowledge, judgment and keenness of perception.

I loved piloting her, though I was ever aware that she had zero tolerance for any major mistake I might make. One serious error of performance or judgment—one inadvertent lack of concentration, and she would destroy me as she was, in turn, devoured by my errors!

She was in love with glorious death. Yet she would live if she could fly as she was designed to do.

Although I never had any close calls with oblivion as I had had in other phases of my flying career, every time I flew her it was a dance with death. She and I both knew it.

How could she be so wonderful and thrilling to pilot under the right conditions, yet so cantankerous and quick to be life threatening under certain operational requirements!

I loved her and respected her totally.

I piloted the Dragon Lady with a love-hate philosophy.

She easily—with full fuel—became airborne in significantly less distance than the length of a football field. She would stretch her elegant black wings and float effortlessly upward.

It was my task to ascertain that her wing tip pogo struts with wheels quickly jettisoned to establish an ambitious climb schedule which carried the Lady and me through 15,000 feet in one minute after liftoff, .a steep angle of climb.

What was not to love in such an amazing aircraft!

She would continue to climb steeply until my Lady and I were out of normal eyesight from the ground. No earthlings could follow her. Was she not my Dragon Lady? She eagerly and gracefully flew through multiple time zones without refueling.

But then she would punish me, would tease me and make me work my buns off to make a high altitude descent and to keep her on terra firma when I attempted to land her. She simply did not want to stop flying!

Such tenacious persistence to remain airborne can be misleading. The U-2 is not a forgiving crème puff that ignores pilot error without serious consequences.

More U-2 fatal accidents than readers probably ever will be aware of have, in some way, resulted from pilot error in a very hostile unforgiving flying environment. Some causative factors, to name but a few, may have resulted from:-70 F outside air temperatures, severe dehydration of the pilot, the bends, pilot overheat from exertion in his space suit, the Armstrong line at approximately 54,000 feet above sea level where water boils at 98.6 F—normal human body temperature

I was protected by a four layered space suit. The outside of this cumbersome garment was simply a protective coating. Inside was a pressure suit and next to my skin a waffle weave underwear. I was plugged in before the flight,—plumbed almost like an octopus—and the limited space was full of telemetry that constantly recorded my heart beat, my blood pressure read by monitors on the ground.

The space suit prevented my blood and other body fluids from boiling off above 54,000 feet when, and if, I should be exposed to the near vacuum of the outside air pressure. That wonderful suit preserved me from dying a bizarre, painful death in approximately one minute—give or take seconds in such a nightmarish survival environment!

I had been flying by this time more than eight hours, much of the time at ultrahigh altitude at an outside air temperature of approximately –70 Fahrenheit. My impervious layered space suit protected me from freezing, incapacitation from the bends, and hypoxia (lack of oxygen)—even death from anoxia (complete loss of oxygen).

That miserably uncomfortable but life-sustaining suit kept me alive. I could peer through the visual lens in front of my space hard hat to constantly watch the instruments, but if I turned my head inside the hard hat, I could see very little. I had to turn my upper torso for better side vision. (This was later improved in updated space suits.)

Then there was always the ever-present specter of violating that altitude related four knot airspeed spread between stall speed with probable engine flameout or structural failure and disintegration of the craft.

When accidents like the above happen, it is unlikely that they would ever be reported accurately or honestly in the ongoing, existing, austere security system that is ever-present with spy aircraft. Men I knew simply disappeared and we would hear much later that they were dead.

This is a paean to the most wonderful aircraft that man has ever invented. Ernest Gann, a writer who captured in enchanted phrases the joy of flying, of aircraft, of pilots and their lives and their obsession for flying, has probably described the world of the U-2 best in his famous book, *The Black Watch*. I can only capture the fascination I personally felt for this vixen of the sky.

I loved her as I had loved no other aircraft, yet I was ever aware of how suddenly the wrong chronology of a series of seemingly insignificant ultra-high altitude events could become lethal.

She was my Dragon Lady—not only mine, but the mutual possession of every U-2 pilot scheduled to fly her. She and her sisters were clones. We could hardly tell one from the other. When I would be hoisted into her tiny cockpit, I would touch her, almost reverently.

I knew my lady very well. That familiarity was life insurance for me. I was always concerned that some unexpected mechanical failure or combination of insignificant minor errors might occur in just the wrong sequence and create an irreversible, disastrous dilemma. That is why I often studied and refreshed my emergency procedures.

Would I pilot her again if I had the opportunity?
In a heartbeat! With eager anticipation!
The Lady was too exciting—too challenging—too fulfilling to ever consider declining any spy pilot's dream of a lifetime! I was never quite sure how or why I had been selected to fly the U-2, but I felt I was one of the chosen each time I flew that fabulous aircraft.

The confining space closed in on me—no more than it had for the past eight hours. Nevertheless, the closer I came to Bodo, the smaller the space around me seemed. As I brought her down, I made a mental note not to recommend this career to any pilot with the slightest history of claustrophobia! It was a good thing we were paid so little, or everyone would have wanted our cushy jobs!

As I descended through 15,000 feet, I put on my business face and attitude—no more reveries! I chased all extraneous thoughts from my mind. It was show time now!

I had a Dragon Lady to coax down onto a runway centerline where she may not wish to land quite yet. I needed to insist that she leave the skies and land, whether she chose to or not!

My requested low pass at 1,000 feet over the runway permitted me to observe the location of all emergency vehicles alongside the duty runway. The emergency vehicles were all strategically positioned at the "ready" in event of serious problems during landing.

The mobile car lights were flashing as the qualified U-2 pilot driving the vehicle awaited my arrival just off the runway threshold. I knew the mobile officer driving the high speed sedan was ready to burn his rubber tires to tuck in behind my Dragon Lady as I glided by his auto at exactly 10 feet above the runway centerline.

This was always standard procedure. The mobile officer would chase the U-2 pilot down the runway and talk him down in two foot increments to touchdown at or near full stall airspeed on the runway centerline. At night, he used a spotlight.

When I landed my Dragon Lady, I then was riding a multimillion dollar bicycle, because the wing pogo sticks with wheels are always jettisoned over the runway immediately after takeoff. The purpose is to reduce wing turbulence and drag, and gross weight, to improve maneuverability and increase aircraft range.

I had to be very alert to keep my very long wings from dragging a wing tip at too much speed while continuing to decelerate my bicycle soon after landing touchdown. When I had decelerated to a minimum speed at which I still could keep my wings level, I then allowed one wing to gently tip over and contact the ground. At that point, the U-2 would decelerate to a complete stop on her bicycle landing gear and one lowered wing tip which slid to a stop on its protective titanium skid plate beneath the wing tip, specifically designed to prevent any serious damage to the wing.

She was like an elegantly vain bird who tapped the ground ever so gently to say, "Here I am. Look how wonderfully I flew!"

After she is on the ground, pogo sticks with wheels would be reinserted into the wing sockets by the ground crew. Then she would be ready to be taxied to her final field position for engine shutdown. That procedure should help everyone appreciate how difficult the U-2 is to land and keep it down after initial runway contact.

Notwithstanding the thorough screening and meticulous consideration of each candidate who volunteered and applied to become a U-2 pilot, only about one third of these excellent aviators actually qualified.

She was safely on the ground, but I was exhausted! I had been awake for more than 12 hours and had flown under stressful conditions for 8 to 9 hours.

Was I done? No! She was through, but I was not.

She needed to be taxied—coaxed—to her parking spot or her assigned hanger. Then I had to be assisted—clumsy space suit and all—out of the crowded cockpit for an urgent recess, hydration, maintenance debriefing concerning aircraft condition and any recommended corrective actions necessary before she could be flown again.

I knew I was in as good physical condition as I could get. Yet I was happy to have the ground crew assist in removing my "weary carcass" from the cockpit of my aircraft. I never knew I would work that hard while sitting down for more than eight hours.

A detailed operations debrief is mandatory and invariably classified.

She and I were spies. Where we went and what we did was not to be discussed, until now, nearly a half a century later. I flew her, or her clones, out of Peshawar, Pakistan; Insurlike, Turkey; Osan, South Korea; Akrotiri, Cyprus; and Alconbury, England; as well as Bodo.

I knew that the two pods under her wings were mounted with photographic equipment or electronic receivers that vacuumed the space beneath her wings in all directions.

Once, and only once, I was privileged to see the magnificent scope of the pictures she and I had taken. Most of the time, whatever it was that she recorded was off loaded to be analyzed by other experts. Our job was to collect the vital information, not to know what that information was or what had been done with it.

Most of the successful U-2 pilot candidates agreed that it was a truly humbling experience to have accrued thousands of pilot hours and have exceptional flight records, only to discover what a technically difficult and unforgiving aircraft the Dragon Lady could be. Nonetheless, most of us were attracted like moths to the flame of a lighted candle. We wanted to give the opportunity our "best shots."

Not quite done with the mission yet: an operations debrief was part and parcel of every mission performed. Ops debriefings were invariably classified and thorough.

It had been more than 10 hours since I had had any solid food. It had been a long, arduous, stressful day.

I could luxuriate now; have a hearty, carefully monitored meal if I desired it. I had planned for a long, hot, steamy bath, but it made me so sleepy as it relieved my sore muscles and aching joints that I decided to abbreviate the bath.

First things first: I was ravenous and needed much hydration. Water never tasted so wonderful.

No longer hungry—no longer thirsty—my aches and stiffness subsiding—I was ready for the arms of Morpheus and eight or more hours of deep slumber.

My last waking thoughts were the beautiful, meaningful words of the late John Gillespie McGee Jr. in his poem, "High Flight."

HIGH FLIGHT
John Gillespie Magee, Jr.

Oh, I have slipped the surly bonds of earth
And danced the skies on laughter-silvered wings.
Sunward I've climbed and joined the tumbling mirth
Of sun-split clouds—and done a hundred things
You have not dreamed of—wheeled and soared and swung
High in the sunlit silence. Hov'ring there
I've chased the shouting wind along and flung
My eager craft through footless halls of air.
Up, up the long delirious burning blue
I've topped the wind-swept heights with easy grace,
Where never lark, or even eagle, flew—;
And, while with silent, lifting mind I've trod
The high untrespassed sanctity of space,
Put out my hand, and touched the face of God

This day, she and I were there—over the Arctic Circle above Scandinavia where I reveled in the untrespassed sanctity of space.

It was there that I truly experienced an epiphany.

It came to me, a clear self-realization of who I was, why I was there, and why there was meaning to my life—a manifestation of why I had always been unafraid to put myself in harm's way to carry out dangerous spying missions to successful conclusions. Of why, when death had been my almost certain lot, I had been able to be quietly calm and do the best I could for my crew and my aircraft.

It had always been for my country—my nation—forever!

And this day it was for my wonderful Dragon Lady.

CHAPTER 27—

GETTING READY TO RETIRE

It was great fun to fly 25 feet above the desert floor
at 450 to 500 knots airspeed
with 50 foot high rooster tails of dust following!

I transferred to the U.S. Naval Missile Center, NAS Point Mugu in California in 1969 for my twilight tour on active duty and was based there for the next four years. I was assigned to the Electronic Warfare Division. This was wise utilization of my flying skills and managerial experience since I was to deal with both civilian engineers and Navy personnel.

I was to be involved with flying "test bed" aircraft that were constantly being modified. I was to make airborne tests on a plethora of novel innovations to improve the status of U. S. electronics.

My job was to test fly all new "black boxes" that were developed at Mugu.

"Black box" is a generic name for any electronic device that improves U. S. capability in delivering armament from an aircraft or ship or a land base, or electronically collecting critical, sensitive information from hostile sources.

One of the more notable tests I flew was with an improved missile guidance system for the Sidewinder Air to Air missile.

I also did airborne tests for the Ship to Ship Harpoon missile. The Harpoon was a lethal missile that could potentially disable or even sink a warship with a direct hit.

On many of my test flights, I had a Harpoon warhead actually installed in my test aircraft. I would fly my aircraft as if I were actually a Harpoon missile. My missile warhead carried all the guidance hardware without the explosives.

It was an interesting assignment. I would fly a trajectory to a point just short of impact with the target. The recording instrumentation on my aircraft gave the project engineers data which allowed them to make invaluable improvements for later modifications.

Another time, I tested a "smart bomb" now widely used in warfare.

We executed 61 test runs 25 feet above the desert floor at 500 knots airspeed near Death Valley. Test runs on a new target detection device thwarted two Russian submarines near Pt. Mugu from collecting any classified data. My aircraft was too low and shielded by mountainous terrain

The Navy took advantage of my piloting skills.

I was always intrigued by airborne tests I made away from the Pacific seacoast back in the hinterlands of the California desert in the vicinity of the blistering hot Death Valley and the Panamint Mountain Range.

Some of the ordnance fuse testing runs I was tasked to fly always gave me my "flat-hatting jollies!"

What fun to fly over a level cleared track only 25 feet above the desert floor at 450 to 500 knots airspeed with 50 foot high rooster tails of dust following my aircraft wake as I blistered across the desert floor!

No one was shooting at me: now that was fun!!

We had legitimate cause to do significant amounts of our electronic emission testing in the remote boondocks. We knew there were Russian submarines lurking and eavesdropping off shore west of Port Hueneme.

We kept precise, accurate records of Russian satellites passing periodically over southern California. When a Soviet Satellite was in a good reception position, we always shut down our emission tests—cat and mouse, the same game I had flown for years.

After the years of excitement, it was often boring. The operational flying at Point Mugu was significantly at a much slower pace that the flying I had done during the previous fifteen years.

NAVAL MISSILE CENTER
POINT MUGU, CALIFORNIA 93041

IN REPLY REFER TO

1020
14 APR 1970

From: Commanding Officer, Naval Missile Center
To: Lieutenant Commander R. S. Beat, USN

Subj: Letter of Appreciation

1. The outstanding manner in which you and your crew executed the EX-45 TDD (Target Detection Device) fly-over tests on 24 and 25 March 1970 is a source of pride to the Naval Missile Center.

2. By your accomplishment of twenty-four test runs during the first day of operations and sixty-one runs on the second day, you completed an effort originally expected to require two weeks. Your precise airmanship allowed early project completion, releasing the NA-3A aircraft for other projects and lowering project costs significantly.

3. It is gratifying to me to take this opportunity to express my personal appreciation and recognition of outstanding performance. You and your crew members performed in the highest tradition of the United States Navy. "Well Done."

L. A. Hopkins

L. A. HOPKINS

This letter of appreciation was one of several commendatory letters I received from the Commanding Officer of the U.S. Naval Missile Center when I was a test pilot for new electronic warfare "black boxes."

However, this slower pace allowed me generous amounts of time to research precisely where my wife Jan and I wished to retire. The Navy had kept us constantly house moving, deploying, cruising, separating, reuniting, involved in wars and armed international crises. It had never been dull.

***At the end of my career, I had four rows of medals from the wide variety
of hazardous assignments that were part of my life.***

Jan had been frugal and had saved enough that we could afford a good
house. The question was where to buy one.

We compiled a "major list" of all the items to be considered in select-
ing our retirement location: annual climate, local civic activities, location of
excellent educational facilities, nearness of military fringe benefits—medical, dental, commissary, military exchanges, property taxes, and local
crime rate to name a few.

We reviewed and discussed these items and many others very carefully. Finally, I proffered three garden spots for Jan to consider.

I had narrowed retirement down to three choices: Capri, off the western coast of Italy; Mauritius, approximately 500 miles east of Madagascar
and 20 degrees south of the Equator in the Indian Ocean; and Camarillo,
California, six miles from the base where I was stationed at NAS, Point
Mugu, California.

Through research, I had quickly learned that there was no land available for sale on Capri and had not been for hundreds of years. So it came

down to Mauritius and Camarillo.

My wife Jan asked only one question: "If we live in Mauritius, how will we ever see our grandchildren?"

So, for the next thirty years, Jan and I have lived in Camarillo, only fifteen miles from our daughter Julie and her husband Jeffrey Simonsgaard, and our two grandsons, Jeffrey Scott and Jackson Kai, in Thousand Oaks.

We are all still there and love it!.

Afterword:

There was a lad who went to sea
And left the shore behind him.
I knew him well, for he was me
And now I can not find him.

...Anonymous

Few men have had as full and satisfying life as I. I loved the Navy and flying. The joys of being airborne; the risks, the excitement, the hazards of being a spy in the sky, all fulfilled innate psychological needs

In addition, I was blessed with excellent parents, good friends, and a superb wife and family. What more could any man ask of life?

Military Medals and Campaign Ribbons Awarded:

R. Scott Beat is the proud owner of six rows of ribbons which stand for the following awards:

First Row: Air Medal (20 awards); Navy Commendation with Combat V; Army Commendation Medal

Second Row: Combat Action Ribbon; Navy Unit Commendation Ribbon; Navy Good Conduct Medal;

Third Row: American Campaign Medal; World War II Victory Medal 1941–46; China Service Medal

Fourth Row: National Defense Service Medal; American Forces Expeditionary Service Medal (4 times awarded); South Vietnamese Air Gallantry Medal

Fifth Row: Republic of Vietnam Service Medal 1965 to 73 (6 times awarded); Republic of Vietnam Campaign Medal, 1960; Navy Expert Rifleman Medal;

Sixth Row: Navy Expert Pistol Shot Medal

Additional but Unofficial Medals: Purple Heart; Navy Bronze Star